GENERATIONAL SELLING TACTICS THAT WORK

To Mike -
Best Wishes +
Many thanks -

[signature]
8/6/12

GENERATIONAL SELLING TACTICS THAT WORK

Quick and Dirty Secrets for Selling to Any Age Group

CAM MARSTON

WILEY

John Wiley & Sons, Inc.

Published by John Wiley & Sons, Inc., Hoboken, New Jersey.

Published simultaneously in Canada.

For general information on our other products and services or for technical support, please contact our Customer Care Department within the United States at (800) 762-2974, outside the United States at (317) 572-3993 or fax (317) 572-4002.

Wiley also publishes its books in a variety of electronic formats. Some content that appears in print may not be available in electronic books. For more information about Wiley products, visit our web site at www.wiley.com.

Library of Congress Cataloging-in-Publication Data:

ISBN 978-1-118-01838-5 (cloth)

ISBN 978-1-118-07808-2 (ebk)

ISBN 978-1-118-07809-9 (ebk)

ISBN 978-1-118-07810-5 (ebk)

Printed in the United States of America

10 9 8 7 6 5 4 3 2 1

*This book is dedicated to those who are in the "people business"
and are looking for new ways to connect with those who
could be or should be their customers.*

*Also to the corporate behemoth that is GE, without whom I would
have never begun down this path of learning the selling preferences
of the different generations. GE trains their people well to be
tough negotiators and demanding clients, but, in the end,
their demanding processes tend to make their vendors better
at what they do. That has certainly been my case.*

*And to the Mellow Mushroom at the corner of Old Shell
and University and Satori Coffee House on Old Shell Road,
where I diligently edited and reedited the manuscript.*

*Finally, I'd be foolish to neglect my wife and my family.
They tolerate dramatic mood swings based on my most recent
client calls, long periods of my being away with clients, and
my calls from the road from exotic locations while they're
slogging away at home in carpool lines and endless swim meets
under the blazing south Alabama sun. Lisa, Reiney, Spencer,
Mackey, and Ivey – thanks for letting me do what I do.
I'm one lucky husband and father.*

CONTENTS

PREFACE

Eight years ago an audience member asked me if my information on the generations could be adjusted to apply to sales. "It makes sense," she said, "that if these generations have such strong biases about their workplaces that they may also have some biases about the sales process." At the time my focus was the generational changes impacting the workplace. "Probably," I said, "But I've not done any research into that." A few months later she called me and said, "Do the research. I want you to come speak to my sales force." Thus began my odyssey into generational biases around sales and discovering specific sales tactics that each generation prefers.

In the audience of this first presentation on generational selling was a gentleman with General Electric (GE), whose responsibility was to educate the entire U.S.-based GE sales force on selling tactics. He liked my presentation and said he found some truth in my content, and not long after that I began touring the country speaking to the GE sales forces across the nation. Those speeches and seminars continue to this day, but now it's not just with GE; it's to a broad spectrum of companies across North America.

Most normal people tend to think of sales and service from a few standard frames of mind:

- If I like my product or service for a certain reason, you will like it for that reason, too. Therefore, I will sell it to you featuring the reasons I like it.

- If I want to learn about a product or service, you will likely want to learn about it the same way. Therefore, I'll assume you'll want to learn about it like I do.

- And if I like a salesperson for one reason or another, you'll probably like the salesperson for those same reasons. Therefore, I'll try to behave like the salesperson I'd like to do business with.

What this creates is salespeople, marketers, and service providers who essentially replicate their own preferences on their customers. And, frankly, sometimes this works, but many times it doesn't.

I've written this book to get you "out of you and into them"—into your customer's frame of mind. I want you to become aware of your generational biases and not to let your biases dominate your sales, marketing, or service processes. It's not too hard, actually, and in the process you'll probably learn something about yourself.

Always remember:

- People do business with people that they like.
- People do business with people they think are like themselves.

This book is written to help you become likable to your different generations of customers and to give you tools and ideas for how to become like your different generations of customers. Are they ways for a Millennial to become like a Boomer? Absolutely; if they know what a Boomer prefers when they're making buying decisions, then that Millennial can adjust to become more like the Boomer. The same with a Mature to a Millennial or a Boomer to an Xer. It works from all generations to the others. The key is being able to get out of your habits and routines and into the preferences of your prospect. Knowing what those preferences are is step one.

Good selling.

ACKNOWLEDGMENTS

Steven James never blinked when I called to tell him Wiley wanted the manuscript in six weeks. He quickly got to work organizing the information, helping craft the chapter outlines, and working with me to organize the jumbled and disparate information in my head. This book exists because of his dogged determination to make sure we met the deadline.

Excellent work, Steven, and thank you very much for your help. Now stand by for whats next. . . .

CHAPTER 1

Selling and the Generations

Making a Connection

A customer's decision to buy is usually about 85 percent emotional and 15 percent rational. In a crowded marketplace with many buying options, the typical consumer spends as much time deciding from *whom* they will buy as they do deciding *what* they will buy. Consumers make the emotional part of their choice based on two qualities that they find (or don't find) in a sales professional: likability and respect. Respect comes from vendors' knowledge of their products, services, and industry, as well as from their experience and accomplishments. But likability can be more elusive, even for the friendliest and most outgoing account executive. It's one of those things that just seems to "be there" with some people and not with others.

A big part of successful selling is the likability factor—one's capacity to consistently establish a connection or rapport with prospects, clients, and customers. Clients need to establish a level of comfort with us before they trust us with significant purchase decisions—or even before they will believe anything we say. That comfort level is expressed in phrases like "He gets me" or "She just knows exactly where I'm coming from" or even—if we're really lucky—"Hey, I *like* this guy!" Sometimes, establishing this connection is easy. We just "hit it off" with a client, especially one with whom we share a common background, age group, or interests. Other times, however, it seems

> A big part of successful selling is the likability factor—one's capacity to consistently establish a connection or rapport with prospects, clients, and customers.

more difficult. We can't seem to find the right "wavelength," or we aren't even "speaking the same language." This happens most often with customers who are of different ages and backgrounds than our own.

While this is frustrating it's also completely normal. It is human nature to sell and communicate based on our own perspectives. We often assume that if we like something for a certain reason, then everyone else probably does, too. If we prefer to learn about and buy products in certain ways, then we assume that most others share those preferences. However, your own perspective and preferences may not always be a good match for your sales prospects, especially when you come from different backgrounds. And today's marketplace is made up of people with various ages, experiences, and personal histories. The marketplace is more diverse than ever, making it highly unlikely that you can just sell to people like yourself. You are selling to everyone. In fact, to be successful, you must be able to connect with and sell to people who are nothing like you. And that means different value sets, different communication preferences, and different selling points.

> *It is human nature to sell and communicate based on our own perspectives.*

> *However, your own perspective and preferences may not always be a good match for your sales prospects, especially when you come from different backgrounds.*

No one can be all things to all people. Nor can a sales professional expect to be every client's best friend. But if an account executive can earn a little likability, it will go a long way toward accomplishing some key steps in the sales process. Likability helps you:

Making The Connection

Get them to listen.

Establish a relationship.

Don't turn them off.

Get the last look.

- *Quickly connect.* Get the client to "lean forward" to at least listen to what you have to say.
- *Establish a relationship.* Help the customer feel comfortable enough so that you can communicate about what he or she really wants.
- *Avoid turning them off.* Avoid inadvertently saying or doing things that make them uncomfortable.
- *Earn the last look.* Ensure that the client comes back to you at the end of a competitive process to give you the last chance to make the sale.

Understanding and being sensitive to a client's background, biases, and preferences—and then treating them appropriately—will go a long way toward achieving these likability goals.

Do: Try to understand how customers' backgrounds affect their buying preferences.

Don't: Assume all your customers prefer to buy the same way you do.

Generational Differences

One of the main factors that differentiates today's consumers, and may be separating you from your customers, is generation or age group. We all see the world through our own generational filter. Each generation has a shared history, common biases, and core beliefs. The experiences of our youth shape our points of view. Moreover, our age and our life stage also dictate some of our needs and preferences. In some cases, the differences between generations are minor, while in others, they could prevent you from closing a sale. Many of the things that will help us "get" our clients come with our ability to understand their generational points of view.

> Many of the things that will help us "get" our clients come with our ability to understand their generational points of view.

Often, our failure to connect with clients—to understand "where they are coming from"—lies in our inability to understand their generational background.

We need to understand how to sell across generational divides rather than allowing these differences to short-circuit that crucial connection to provide the best service to our clients. Appreciating generational dynamics provides a way for you to find common ground with clients from all generations and present the information they want in the manner they want it. Whether you are selling financial services, home appliances, cars, or smartphones, generational preferences can make a difference. Understanding clients' age-based points of view is an indispensable soft skill that you can use to establish the connection and make the sale.

Generational Fact

Surveys and market research have shown that different generations have very distinct views about products, politics, religion, careers, and just about everything else. Generation is one of the most important factors that shape people's opinions and views.

We're all familiar with the typical traits that separate generations, such as hairstyles, vocabulary, music, and clothing. Others, however, are not as easily identifiable, especially when it comes to their behavior as consumers. For example, some generations are inclined to take sales professionals at their word; others won't believe a word you say. Some are impressed by professional credentials, while others are turned off by them. One generation usually wants standard offerings. Another wants everything customized. Still another wants to know that you have a Plan B ready in case Plan A doesn't work out. Each of these approaches has a distinct generational appeal, and we need to know when and how to use them.

Sending the wrong generational signals can significantly alienate clients. Sales techniques that are effective for one generation may come off as "pushy" for another, whereas approaches that work with older generations may identify you as

Sales techniques that are effective for one generation may come off as "pushy" for another, whereas approaches that work with older generations may identify you as "like my parents" for younger customers.

"like my parents" for younger customers. Methods of communication that seem normal to you might be perceived as intrusive by members of a different age group. These are all examples of potential generation gaps in the relationship between you and your clients that could cost you a sale that you are otherwise well positioned to make.

The Four Generations

Generational differences are more significant in marketing and selling now than at any time in our history. For one thing, there currently are more generations alive and active than ever before, as modern medicine and affluence have produced a revolution in longevity. People are living longer than they ever have, and are remaining healthy and active much later into their lives. They are working past traditional retirement age and continuing to be active consumers into their 70s and 80s. To illustrate this with one statistic, consider that the fastest-growing population segment today is 85 and over!

Because our modern world has changed so quickly and in so many ways, each successive generation has had a significantly different experience growing up. Coming of age in the 1940s was totally different from growing up in the 1960s which, in turn, was nothing like growing up in the 1980s, which was completely dissimilar from the 2000s. This has resulted in four generations with four very distinct experiences—and vastly unique generational personalities.

Finally, the importance of younger generations in the marketplace has grown significantly over the years that span these four age groups. While young people had little or no

Generational Fact

The four generations in today's marketplace are:

Matures: Born before 1946
Baby Boomers: Born between 1946 and 1964
Generation X: Born between 1965 and 1979
Millennials: Born between 1980 and 2000

spending power or much influence on purchasing decisions 60 or 70 years ago, younger generations today have more influence and disposable income. Teens and 20-somethings are very active consumers in almost every market; and they are among the leading consumers in some cases, such as mobile technology.

> While young people had little or no spending power or much influence on purchasing decisions 60 or 70 years ago, younger generations today have more influence and disposable income.

They also wield tremendous influence over the spending habits of older generations in their circle of family and friends. These youngest consumers—who at one time participated in the marketplace only in a limited way or through their parents—are now as active and influential as any other generation, and in some cases, even more so.

So what does all of this mean? In short, that the marketplace's landscape has changed significantly just over our lifetimes. For the first time, we have four distinct and important generations of consumers to whom we must market and sell. This means that it's now more important than ever before for sales professionals to understand the following four generations in today's marketplace:

- Matures: Born before 1946
- Baby Boomers: Born between 1946 and 1964
- Generation X: Born between 1965 and 1979
- Millennials: Born between 1980 and 2000

Each of these generations has shared experiences and characteristics, and each presents distinct challenges and opportunities to sales and marketing professionals. Specific selling tactics are effective for each one. Of course, generational biases are not ironclad, and birth date does not dictate personality. Many factors and influences comprise a consumer's makeup. Naturally, professionals who are involved in marketing and sales must first develop a thorough knowledge of the products and services they offer, an understanding of their industry's competitive landscape, and a solid grasp of marketing and selling principles. But even well-equipped account executives, managers, and sales professionals can be handicapped by a lack of generational insight. The fact is that the generation of which you are a member makes a difference for you, both as a sales professional and a consumer. And recognizing and understanding the differences between generations can be a very effective tool for the sales professional.

> *Naturally, professionals who are involved in marketing and sales must first develop a thorough knowledge of the products and services they offer, an understanding of their industry's competitive landscape, and a solid grasp of marketing and selling principles.*

The study and definition of these generations is part of the study of demography, or population trends. Demographers and market researchers have always analyzed and labeled different generations, often marked by a large increase or decrease in birth rates over a period of time. We are particularly interested in the last four generations of the twentieth century for two reasons:

1. These four represent very significant population shifts with deep and long-lasting effects on society and commerce.
2. All four are still alive and active in our society and, therefore, active in the marketplace. In other words, they are all potential customers.

Developing an understanding of each of these generations and their differences is essential to a professional's toolkit, especially when it comes to selling and marketing *across* generational lines. We'll describe each generation in detail later in the book, but let's take a quick look at each of them:

The Matures: Born before 1946, the Matures are really a composite generation of several groups, all born before the end of World War II. These include the Veterans, also known as the Greatest or G.I. Generation (born before

Generational Fact

The Baby Boomer and Millennial generations are the two largest generations in American history.

1925), and the Silent Generation (born between 1925 and 1945). These generations have played important roles in our history and are known for their sense of sacrifice, patriotism, and duty. Almost all Matures have reached retirement age today. However, due to increases in life expectancy, they are much more active in the marketplace and the workplace than previous generations were at this stage in life. There are about 40 million Matures—also known as Traditionalists or Traditionals—in the United States in 2011.

> *However, due to increases in life expectancy, they are much more active in the marketplace and the workplace than previous generations were at this stage in life.*

The Baby Boomers: Born between 1946 and 1964, the Baby Boomers get their name from the remarkable "boom" in the birthrate following World War II. Over 76 million American children were born during that time. As this exceptionally large generation has moved through each life stage, it has reshaped ideas about youth, education, work, and aging. Baby Boomers have always had a sense of their generation's uniqueness and importance. They maintain a lifelong connection to their youth in the 1960s, a time of momentous cultural and political change. Baby Boomers are known for their optimism, self-confidence, and ambition. Their numbers have been supplemented by immigration, and they now total nearly 80 million Americans. Until the emergence of the Millennials, Baby Boomers were considered the most important demographic in commerce, marketing, and sales.

> *Baby Boomers are known for their optimism, self-confidence, and ambition.*

Generation X: Born between 1965 and 1979, Generation X was originally known as the "baby bust" due to the decline in birth rates that resulted from birth control's wide availability during the 1960s. They get their name from a novel about the generation that was published in the 1990s. Gen Xers grew up with less economic and family security than the Boomers, often in households with divorced or two working parents. The previous generation's optimism gave way to the scandals, inflation, world crises, and recessions of the 1970s and 1980s. Xers are thus known as skeptical, cynical, and pessimistic. Despite being labeled "slackers" in their youth, Xers generally shoulder the responsibility for their own well-

> *Despite being labeled "slackers" in their youth, Xers generally shoulder the responsibility for their own well-being.*

being. The advent of the personal computer and Internet during their youth made them the first tech-savvy generation. They number about 60 million in the United States today.

Millennials: Born between 1980 and 2000, Millennials were originally known as the "Echo Boom" because they represent a surge in the number of births that came mainly as a result of the Baby Boomer generation having children of their own. They have lived for most of their youth in a time of broad economic and technological expansion. Indeed, ease with technology and telecommunication is one of the hallmarks of Millennials, along with a sense of optimism and entitlement that comes from growing up in an "everybody wins" world that their very attentive parents carefully structured and programmed. Millennials are also known for their sense of social and environmental responsibility, their responsiveness to peers and trendsetters, and their

Generational Fact

Demographics is the study of population trends that market researchers use to find target markets for products and services. Demographers identify and define age groups by their characteristics and preferences and identify them with generational labels.

consumption of new media. They number about 85 million in the United States and are beginning to eclipse Generation X in spending power. They are sometimes also known as Generation Y, because they are successors to X, or Generation Next.

> They number about 85 million in the United States and are beginning to eclipse Generation X in spending power.

You may already notice some differences in this brief introduction. It is immediately clear, for instance, that some generations are much larger than others. Substantial increases or decreases in birth rates and surges in population are part of what defines generations. The large size of certain generations, like the Baby Boomers and the Millennials, is what makes them so influential in the marketplace.

> Older generations are the richest because they have spent a lifetime accumulating wealth during a time of increasing prosperity. However, since younger generations grew up during that same time of prosperity, they are more accustomed to affluence—even if they didn't have to work for it.

Another significant difference between generations is wealth. Older generations are the richest because they have spent a lifetime accumulating wealth during a time of increasing prosperity. However, since younger generations grew up during that same time of prosperity, they are more accustomed to affluence—even if they didn't have to work for it. That affluence has allowed these younger individuals to stay young longer. They've been able to put off adult decisions like marriage, children, and careers until they are well into adulthood—much later than their counterparts from older generations did.

These broad demographic factors like size and wealth are some of the elements that shape each generation's attitudes, as well as some extensive differences in each one's outlook. For example, older groups tend to be the "We" generations who are more oriented to the needs of their society or team—whether it's their colleagues, family, community, or country. The younger generations are more "Me"-centric and focused on individual needs. The "We" generations grew up in times of struggle, hard work, and competition, while the "Me" generations came of age in kinder, gentler times of affluence. From the old-

> *The "We" generations grew up in times of struggle, hard work, and competition, while the "Me" generations came of age in kinder, gentler times of affluence.*

est Mature to the youngest Millennial, almost everyone in the marketplace today fits somewhere on this "We to Me" continuum.

Other important features that shape generations are the formative experiences that each generation experiences as they come of age. Matures always remember the struggles of the Depression and World War II, whereas Baby Boomers were brought up during the Cold War and came of age during the tumult of the 1960s. Generation X was often left on its own—by parents' divorces and economic necessity—and

Generational Fact

Factors that Shape the Generations

- **Formative experiences:** Major events and developments they experienced growing up.
- **Life stage:** Their current age and the phase of life they are going through today.

was disillusioned by scandals like Watergate and disasters like the *Challenger* space shuttle. Millennials were raised during the tech revolution and prosperity of the 1990s, but had their security threatened by events like Columbine and 9/11. These kinds of episodes tend to stay in a generation's memory and shape its members' personalities over a lifetime; they can make it more cautious or bold, optimistic or skeptical, thrifty or extravagant. All of these characteristics help determine each generation's behavior in the marketplace.

Finally, an important part of each generation's personality is its current life stage; in other words, how old they are and how their age affects their lifestyles. Matures, for example, are over 65, so many are retired. They have accumulated a lot of wealth from a lifetime of work in a prosperous time, but may be inclined to preserve their resources for retirement and medical expenses, or for their heirs. Baby Boomers now range in age from their 40s to their 60s, and many are in the prime of their careers as executives and decision makers. Some younger Boomers especially are now "sandwiched" between caring for their children and their aging parents. Members of Generation X have settled into career and family life, are buying homes, and have several decades of prime earning years ahead. Millennials are in college and early careers and are just beginning to start families. Each life stage entails certain responsibilities and lifestyles that affect how each generation behaves as consumers.

While demographics, formative experiences, and life stage are some of the key factors in determining a generation's character traits and tendencies, this is not to say that they determine every individual member's personality. Everyone is born with his or her own DNA, none of which is determined by generation. Obviously, it's also possible—and almost guaranteed—that any two people from the same generation can have different experiences and outlooks. For example, someone born in 1964 is likely to have a very different upbringing than someone born in 1946, even though they are both technically Baby Boomers. However, using some basic sociology and common sense, it is definitely possible to observe and draw some general conclusions about the characteristics of each generation that will apply more often than not. And with some basic knowledge about each generation's characteristics and attitudes—combined with some common sense—we can apply

> And with some basic knowledge about each generation's characteristics and attitudes—combined with some common sense—we can apply this insight to marketing and selling in ways that improve our performance.

this insight to marketing and selling in ways that improve our performance.

Generational Insight for Selling

The first step in applying generational tactics in selling is to learn about the generations by becoming familiar with each one's characteristics, likes, and dislikes. This basic working knowledge will help you begin to tailor the appeal of your company, product/service, and yourself to fit each generation to whom you sell or want to sell. This book will provide you with a basic snapshot of each of the four generations to assist you in learning each one. These snapshots will arm you with the knowledge you need to identify and recognize each generation in the marketplace and choose the most appropriate generational marketing and selling tactics.

The next step is recognizing these generational characteristics in your customers—insight that you can apply in two ways. One is very broad and poses questions like: From what generations are your customers? What generations do you want as your clients? Does what you say about yourself, your organization, and your products and services convey the right generational messages to the clients you have as well as the ones you want? The second application is more specific, and requires that you consider things like: From what generation is the customer standing in front of you? Of what generation is the customer you are about to call a member?

Sometimes it's easy to answer these questions. You'll realize when you're addressing broad matters about your product or service's appeal that certain items are clearly more attractive to certain generations. For example, offerings related to retirement have obvious appeal for older generations, whereas the natural market for items like video game gadgets are younger generations.

However, many products are not restricted by generational appeal, or at least they shouldn't be. Some, like financial services and appliances, should interest all generations. And there are still other cases in which items are associated with one generation or another, but really should not be limited to those markets. For instance, while retirement savings companies are usually associated with older generations, young people can—and should—be concerned about their retirement, too. By the same token, we often think of smartphones as toys or gadgets for the young, but their use among older generations is expanding rapidly.

How can you get more information about your business's generational appeal? One easy way is to take advantage of resources that are accessible to everyone. Market research is available for almost every category of product and service, and is even broken down by age or even generational category in most cases. Organizations like Nielsen and Forrester conduct research for a variety of industries, and often publish their results in press releases or articles that appear in popular magazines like *Forbes* or *Advertising Age*, or on Web sites like MartketWatch.com. In other cases, industry-specific research is available in trade journals, or through trade or professional associations. Groups like the National Association of Realtors or the National Auto Dealers Association, for example, regularly conduct such investigations and make them available to their members or sell it to interested parties. Even data available through the U.S. Census or survey groups like Pew or Gallup may be relevant to your industry.

> *Market research is available for almost every category of product and service, and is even broken down by age or even generational category in most cases. Organizations like Nielsen and Forrester conduct research for a variety of industries, and often publish their results in press releases or articles that appear in popular magazines like* Forbes *or* Advertising Age, *or on Web sites like MartketWatch.com.*

To Do

Some quick and easy generational market research:

1. Conduct an Internet search for surveys and research about your industry that breaks consumers down by generation.

2. Consult your industry's trade publications and professional and trade organizations.

3. Compile age data on your customers from your company's existing paperwork on them (if you have it).

4. Solicit generational data on customer feedback, mailing list, and promotional giveaway forms.

5. Commission a survey from a market research firm.

Finding existing generational market research has gotten a lot easier in recent years thanks to tools like search engines and the World Wide Web. Often, simple searches using sites like Google or Bing will turn up current market data relevant to your business. You can simply type your product, service, or industry's name into the search box along with another key word. For example, if you search for "financial services Baby Boomers" you will find many Web pages that address Boomers' interest in financial services. Even better—click the "News" tab of Google or Bing to see recent stories, news items, and press releases that mention Baby Boomers *and* financial services. You may have to scroll through a few Web pages to find what you are looking for, but you can quickly narrow the results by adding the words *survey, market research,* or *poll* to your search—as in *baby boomers financial services survey*. This will lead you to some data you can use in many cases. You can then try it with the names of the other generations. While it may take some time to enter the various combinations of search terms and scroll through the results, the potential benefit is *100 percent free* market research. Following these sorts of surveys and polls will also allow you to detect changes in the marketplace as the generational personalities evolve over time.

If you cannot seem to find what you need to know from Internet searches, trade publications, and professional associations, you can easily create your own generational market research. If appropriate to your needs and budget, you can simply commission some generational market research from a consultant or firm that specializes in just that. The Market Research Association (www.mra-net.org) and similar organizations can provide you with a list of reputable companies that provide such services.

In many cases, a simpler and cheaper approach will do just fine: just do it yourself. Use some straightforward techniques to gather data from your customers or clients. After all, who better to provide data about your clientele than your current customers themselves? In fact, you may already have existing age data for your customers in paperwork that simply needs to be analyzed and categorized. If not, just request generational data from your customers in the course of doing business with them through techniques and occurrences like:

- Feedback and comment forms
- When gathering typical data at the point of sale

- When collecting data for mailing and e-mail lists
- On customer information forms
- Through promotional giveaways

Unless it is absolutely necessary for your particular business, it is best *not* to ask for your clients' birth dates.

> *Unless it is absolutely necessary for your particular business, it is best not to ask for your clients' birth dates.*

Privacy and identity theft concerns make that seem too intrusive. It's probably best not to ask them their specific age, because as we know, many people are sensitive about revealing that, too. The best way to gather this information is to include a list of age ranges for them to select from, like this:

Age Range

- 19–31
- 32–46
- 47–65
- 66 and over

This will tell you exactly what generation they fit into without having to ask for too much personal information. Of course, you should update the age ranges as these groups age over time—the dates here are accurate as of 2011. Then, when you've collected a decent number of responses, you will have your own generational market research!

Once you know who your customers are—and, just as importantly, who they aren't—you'll be able to use your generational knowledge to best position and portray your business to reach the markets you want. Of course, target marketing, product positioning, and image are usually the marketing department's concerns, while we are primarily concerned with selling tactics here. However, you will want to be sure that the way in which you market your products and services puts you in a position to sell them across generational lines. And at a minimum, you want to know to whom you are selling and you could be selling. Some basic market research and genera-

> *And at a minimum, you want to know to whom you are selling and you could be selling.*

tional positioning will create opportunities for sales. Later in the book, in the chapters on each generation, we'll show you how to position and portray your business for each of them.

The other component of identifying your clients' generations has to do with recognizing the generational characteristics of the customer who is right in front of you in a potential sales situation. Again, it may be easy in some cases. You may already know their age, since it might be on a form they have filled out or simply something they mentioned. It might be fairly obvious when meeting someone to get a rough idea of what generational category he or she fits into, while you may not be sure in other cases. Many people look and act younger or older

> *Many people look and act younger or older than they really are.*

than they really are. Of course, the *last* thing you want to do is to start a conversation with a sales prospect by asking how old they are—or assuming that you know! When you are unsure, you can use some clues to select the appropriate generational approach. Let's say you are meeting with a youngish client but can't really figure out if they are Generation X or Millennial. Does he have tattoos, or is she

Do: Use your generational knowledge along with the customer's visual, behavioral, and verbal clues to select the appropriate generational selling tactics.

Don't: Ask your client's age or birth date, unless there is a valid business reason to do so. Older clients may feel sensitive about the issue, and younger clients will see it as an invasion of their privacy. And never assume that you can "tell" how old a client is.

constantly sending text messages? If so, it's probably best to go with the Millennial approach. Or perhaps you are visiting a client who could be a Boomer or a Gen Xer. Does he or she have a wall of plaques and certificates? Go with the Boomer tactics.

Finally, if the visual clues don't give away a customer's generation, you might be able to ask a couple of questions during your conversation that will tell you what you need to know. Questions like "Should I call or text?," "Are you on Facebook?," or "Do anything interesting last weekend?" might give you the hints you need to adopt the right generational approach. In this book, in the segments on each generation, we'll provide the keys to the visual, behavioral, and verbal clues that will steer you in the right generational direction.

Generational Selling Tactics

Once you know who your customers are in terms of their generations, you can begin to use generational selling tactics.

This approach simply entails the things that you say and do during the sales process that put your clients at ease and make them comfortable with you—methods that help you to make the connection. In some cases, knowing a client's generational biases will help you choose from among traditional selling tactics. For example, should you emphasize the sizzle or the steak? Should you push this sale toward a close or should you back off? A customer's generation will help answer these questions for you.

There are specific generational approaches in other instances that are effective. For example, Matures will feel reassured and comfortable if you show them your credentials, awards, and positive reviews, whereas Gen Xers will only feel reassured when you show them a clean criminal background check and your company's audited financial statement. While that's probably a bit of an exaggeration, the very real point is that each approach will have a very different effect depending on your customers' generations. You want to know with whom you are dealing and choose the appropriate openings and closings and keep things smooth in between.

> *You want to know with whom you are dealing and choose the appropriate openings and closings and keep things smooth in between.*

In the chapters ahead, we'll provide you with a clear snapshot of each of the four generations. These snapshots will walk you through each generation's experiences and mind-set. We'll cover them in order of importance to the marketplace, starting with the biggest spending generation, the Baby Boomers, followed by the largest generation, the Millennials. Then we'll cover the generation that is just now entering its earning peak, Generation X, and finally the generation with the highest per-capita net worth, the

Matures. What are their characteristics, likes, and dislikes? Why are they important? How do you recognize them when you meet them? What, when, where, why, and how do they buy? These chapters will help you learn the generations so that you can choose appropriate tactics for each generational selling situation.

In the chapters that follow each generational snapshot, we will give you some hands-on selling tactics for each generation. What do you need to do and say to make a connection with each generation of client? What should you *not* do and say? How does each generation prefer to communicate with sales professionals? What are the best approaches to closing the sale with each generation?

Arming yourself with a working knowledge of the four generations—and the best selling tactics to use with each—will give you a competitive edge in some key areas of selling, especially in establishing and maintaining a relationship and a comfort level with your clients and customers. That edge might earn you the last look or opportunity for a sale—or even the sale itself. And it just might earn you some loyal repeat customers and some glowing referrals. Those are the benefits of generational insight that no sales professional should be without.

> *That edge might earn you the last look or opportunity for a sale—or even the sale itself.*

Snapshot of Baby Boomers

Meet the Baby Boomers

The Baby Boomers are the wealthiest generation in American history. They were born between 1946 and 1964 and now number about 80 million. Today, the Boomers are in control. They run our local, state, and national governments. They are the bosses, supervisors, managers, and CEOs of most companies. They dominate the workforce because of their enormous numbers and, through their intense work ethic and competitive nature, the Boomers moved productivity in the United States to the forefront of the world. Boomers are still working as hard as they've ever worked, but, lately, some are asking if their intense work ethic has paid off in the way they had hoped. They are still evolving today. Older Boomers are nearing retirement and even younger Boomers are now confronting the challenges of aging. As they evolve into this new life stage, they will continue to reshape every aspect of life they touch.

> *The Baby Boomers are the wealthiest generation in American history.*

Baby Boomer Fact

The Baby Boomers were the largest generation of children born in the United States.

Baby Boomers were the original "Me" generation. They were born in the years following World War II into a world

29

where children were to be "seen and not heard." As they became teenagers and young adults, they made it clear that they would be heard. Because of the size of the generation, Boomers shifted the country's focus to youth in the 1950s and 1960s. As they grew up, they began to question and challenge traditional values and ways of life. At the same time, the size of the generation offered a potential bonanza to manufacturers, marketers, and media companies. At almost 80 million strong, they were too important a demographic to ignore.

The emergence of the Boomers coincided with changes in modern life that would help shape them and that they, in turn, would help to shape. During their youth, for the first time in history, almost every family had a car and a television, enabling the growth of suburbs and mass media—both of which helped define the Boomer experience. They grew up in a time of unprecedented prosperity, when the United States became the world's unquestioned dominant economic power. In the relatively safe, comfortable, and prosperous environment of the postwar United States, when progress and technology were on the march, they came to believe anything was possible. At the top of their list was changing and improving the world around them, even if everyone else thought they were too young to get involved or have a say. They created the nation's first distinct "youth culture." In that culture, questioning the established way of doing things became part of their identity. In the classic 1955 film *Rebel without a Cause*, one of the first movies about Baby Boomers, James Dean's character is told by his father, "You'll learn when you're older," to which he replies, "I don't think I want to learn that way."

Rebel without a Cause was supposed to be an exposé of the Boomers' youthful moral decay, but its producers surely knew who was lining up to buy tickets. It was a runaway hit and James Dean became a Boomer hero. As a market for music, movies, and television, the Boomers represented a once in a lifetime opportunity. Despite the fact that older generations generally disapproved of the young Boomers' taste in pop culture, media executives and marketers were keen to capitalize on it. The youth culture turned into the youth market and the youth market became the most important demographic in the marketplace. It still is.

As the Baby Boomers matured into young adults,

> *The youth culture turned into the youth market and the youth market became the most important demographic in the marketplace. It still is.*

college students, and draftees for the Vietnam War, they became even more assertive about their views and their tastes. The youth culture became known as the "counterculture," complete with its own music, fashion, and hairstyles. "Don't trust anyone over 30," professional hippie and protestor Jerry Rubin famously proclaimed, and it became the slogan of generational flower power. While many earnest Boomers joined "the Movement" to fight injustice, most others were more interested in the lifestyle. By the late 1960s, marketers were enthusiastically catering to that lifestyle. Most major studios and clothing makers set up youth divisions. Blue jeans, sandals, and tie-dyed shirts became fashionable for everyone. Rock-and-roll topped the charts. One observer of the counterculture compared the day's rock stars to the titans of industry, saying, "The only difference between a rock king and a robber baron is six inches of hair."

Even though the majority of voters did not support the agenda of "the Movement," Baby Boomers, through their sheer numbers and cultural power, were able to effect some changes. In the face of the vociferous opposition of young people, Lyndon Johnson declined to seek reelection as

Baby Boomer Fact

In 1966, the Baby Boom generation was named *Time* magazine's "Man of the Year."

president, and the nation began to back away from its engagement in Vietnam. The voting age was lowered to 18, enabling many more Boomers to vote at a younger age. The Boomers had the attention of the nation. In 1966, *Time* named the Baby Boom generation as its "Man of the Year." They came to believe that anything was possible if they set their minds and hard work to it. It's an attitude they have held onto as the years have gone by.

The Baby Boomers were the first generation to delay the milestones of adulthood, putting off marriage and family until well into their 20s, going to and staying in college longer than previous generations, and delaying the start of their careers. Once they finally embraced adulthood, they proved to be ambitious, entrepreneurial, and hardworking. At work, they have been enthusiastic to the point of workaholic. In the 1970s and 1980s, the hippies became the yuppies. They retained their idealism but put most of their efforts into enjoying the finer things in life. They became enthusiastic consumers. In adulthood they have dom-

> *In adulthood they have dominated the marketplace as much as they did in their youth.*

inated the marketplace as much as they did in their youth. They started families, albeit smaller ones than their parents, and gave birth to the Millennial generation. They want to be devoted parents whose kids lack for nothing. They tend to raise their kids as their friends and want them to have every bit of attention, every valuable experience, and every trendy plaything they can afford them.

Baby Boomer Fact

The median buyer of Harley Davidson motorcycles is a Baby Boomer.

Today, the Boomers are at the peak of their careers and in leadership roles in most industries and businesses. They now have over $2 trillion in annual spending power. Older Boomers are near-

> *They now have over $2 trillion in annual spending power.*

ing retirement, and younger Boomers are planning for it. They still carry their youthful enthusiasm, optimism, and idealism with them, along with a powerful sense of nostalgia for their groundbreaking youth. They are intent on staying young and keeping the flame alive. Now, their mind-set has been challenged by recent hard economic times, and they are gradually adapting to new technologies that come more easily to younger generations. Still, they continue to be one of the most important demographics in history and in the market-place. Like the pig passing through the snake, their presence and impact is obvious in each stage of life they pass through.

Baby Boomers: The Demographics

Born: 1946–1964
Population: 80 million
Spending power: Over $2 trillion
Largest generation of children born in the United States
Wealthiest generation in U.S. history

Who Are the Baby Boomers?

The Baby Boomers are the children of the generations that make up the Matures, specifically the Veterans (born 1901–1924) and the Silent Generation (born 1925–1945). The Baby Boomers represented just what their name suggests, a "boom" or surge in birth rates that started immediately after World War II and continued into the 1960s. Following a decline in birth rates through the Great Depression and World War II, returning veterans had the urge to start new families and settle into quiet, domestic lives. The environment in postwar America encouraged these developments further through the G.I. Bill, the development of suburbs, advances in medicine, and long-lasting economic prosperity. The number of the births in the 1940s was 33 percent higher than in the 1930s, most of that increase coming after the war. By 1954, U.S. births reached the 4 million mark for the first time in history and stayed at that level for a decade. By 1957, the birth rate reached a level of almost four children per family! By 1965, 40 percent of the nation's population was under 20 years of age.

Today, Baby Boomers number about 80 million in the United States. Their numbers have been supplemented by immigration. They range in age from their mid-40s to mid-60s. The oldest Boomers hit the traditional retirement

Baby Boomer Fact

In 1965, Baby Boomers made up 40 percent of the population. Today, they make up over a quarter of the population.

age of 65 in 2011, reaching that age at a rate of one every 10 seconds. Many of the youngest Boomers are still raising children. Because of their size and varying experiences, the Baby Boomers are often divided into two groups: early and late.

> *Because of their size and varying experiences, the Baby Boomers are often divided into two groups: early and late.*

The early cohort, born between 1946 and 1954, is often known as Leading Edge Boomers or simply Early Boomers. The latter group, born between 1955 and 1964 are called Trailing Edge Boomers, Late Boomers, or Generation Jones. The distinction between these groups of Boomers can be an important one. To begin with, they had some different experiences. For example, late Boomers are the ones who didn't go to Woodstock because they couldn't drive yet, and it would have kept them up past their bedtimes anyway. More importantly, the extremes of the two groups are at different life stages. One is getting ready to retire, and the other is still getting kids ready for school every morning. In the chapter on Boomer selling tactics, we'll discuss how certain businesses may want to treat these groups slightly differently.

In general, Boomers have reached the peak of their careers and are in leadership and management positions. Because of their work ethic and because they have enjoyed long careers during times of strong economic growth, they have accumulated enormous spending power, estimated at over $2 trillion per year. That is a stunning figure, but it represents the earnings of the most significant generation in history through a lifetime of work in the most prosperous time in American history. Among the most successful and notable Baby Boomers are U.S presidents Bill Clinton and George W. Bush, Microsoft founder Bill Gates, boxing icon

Muhammad Ali, basketball legends Larry Bird and Magic Johnson, movie producer Steven Spielberg, director Oliver Stone, and actor Sylvester Stallone.

Following the recession of 2008–2009, many Boomers are revising their financial and retirement plans. Boomers were the hardest-hit generation by the recession in terms of losses to their savings, investments, and retirement accounts. Many are planning to work well beyond traditional retirement age because of financial concerns. Others want to continue to work because they are still physically and mentally vibrant and enjoy what they do. They are keen to put off "old age" as long as possible and typically think of themselves as 10 to 15 years younger than they are. The medical revolution in longevity will enable them to continue to live and pursue their careers and interests longer than any previous generation. As long as they have anything to say about it, they are here to stay. In a popular phrase from their youth, they plan to "keep on truckin'."

> *They are keen to put off "old age" as long as possible and typically think of themselves as 10 to 15 years younger than they are.*

Why Are They Called Baby Boomers?

Baby Boomers get their name from the demographic facts: they were born during the biggest "boom" or surge in the birth rate in history. Demographers noticed the trend immediately. In 1948, *Newsweek* recognized its economic importance in the headline "Population: Babies Mean Business." By 1951, newspapers were already using the term *boom* to describe the rise in births. The name stuck and became

What's In A Name?

Baby Boomers are called that because they born during a "boom" or surge in live births. Early Baby Boomers (born 1946–1954) are sometimes called Leading Edge Boomers. Late Baby Boomers (born 1955–1964) are sometimes called Trailing Edge Boomers or Generation Jones.

increasingly common. By the 1970s and 1980s, Boomers were proudly using the label to describe their generation. Previously labeled as hippies or flower children for their counterculture, they have come to be known universally by the remarkable rise in births of which they were a part. They are the Baby Boomers, and they are proud of it.

When Were They Born?

Short answer: between 1946 and 1964. Some demographers trace the beginning of the rise in births to as early as 1944 and others date the beginning of the end of the Boom as early as 1961. None of these interpretations has gained much popular traction. In fact, the U.S. Census uses the dates of 1946–1964 to officially define the Baby Boom generation, and so does just about everyone else. The only other important dates to remember are those that are sometimes used to divide the Baby Boom into sections: the Leading Edge Boomers (born 1946–1954) and the Trailing Edge Boomers, called Generation Jones (born 1955–1964).

Formative Experiences

Baby Boomers: The Formative Experiences

The Cold War and the Red Scare

The Civil Rights Movement

The Vietnam War, the draft, and antiwar protests

Assassinations of John F. Kennedy, Martin Luther King, Jr., and Robert F. Kennedy

Woodstock

1968 Democratic Convention

The Pill and the Sexual Revolution

Roe v. Wade

Watergate

Baby Boomers grew up in a world that had been transformed by the experience of World War II and its aftermath. The tensions of the Cold War and the Red Scare stoked fears of communism and nuclear nightmare. At the same time, the nation was experiencing booming prosperity and new wealth, which benefitted Boomers' families. Starting in the 1950s, the Civil Rights movement began to challenge the country's status quo, and race-related issues were a source of controversy for decades. In 1963, the nation was shocked by the assassination of President John F. Kennedy. That tragedy remains the single most memorable shared event of many Boomers' lives. Unfortunately, it was followed a few years later by the assassinations of Martin Luther King, Jr., and Robert F. Kennedy, and the nation seemed to be in turmoil. No issues were more prominent or divisive in the Boomers' youth than the Vietnam War and the draft. Together, events like antiwar protests and civil rights demonstrations, like the demonstrations at the 1968 Democratic Convention, galvanized most of the Boomer generation against the values of their parents. The counterculture made the Haight-Ashbury district of San Francisco its unofficial capital, a beacon to flower children around the country. Around 1964, the birth control pill became widely legal and available, triggering changes in sexual mores. In 1969, the Woodstock music festival, billed as "Three days of peace and music," seemed to embody everything that the generation stood for.

As the Boomers' became young adults, Watergate seemed to confirm their worst suspicions about authority. The Supreme Court's 1973 *Roe v. Wade* decision seemed like an extension of the trend toward personal and moral freedom but has been a source of bitter division and controversy ever since. Boomer heroes like Jimi Hendrix and Janis Joplin died of drug overdoses, casting a pall on the Boomers' freewheeling lifestyle. The Boomers gradually grew up, eventually embracing the American dream and the affluence that it promised, becoming the "yuppies" (shorthand for "young, urban professional") of the 1980s. They never quite gave up on their idealism, optimism, or their belief that they could

> *The Boomers gradually grew up, eventually embracing the American dream and the affluence that it promised, becoming the "yuppies" (shorthand for "young, urban professional") of the 1980s.*

change the world, as evidenced by events like the 1985 "We are the World" concert and video, an effort to end hunger in Africa that featured Boomer standbys like Bob Dylan and Bruce Springsteen. Nor were they willing to put their youth behind them. Instead, they celebrated it in nostalgic movies like *The Big Chill* while they dramatized the trauma of their own aging in TV shows like *thirtysomething*.

The experiences of the Boomers' youth and the memories of it are the source of a very strong generational bond, comparable to the uniting effect of the Great Depression and World War II on Matures. The experiences of the 1960s, in particular, have come to define the generation. Although the ideals and the movements of the generation during that time never quite achieved the goals they had in mind, many Boomers still remember them fondly. Most have moved on to serious, successful professional lives but the "Age of Aquarius" will always be a part of them.

Baby Boomers: The Life Stage

Baby Boomers range in age from their mid-40s to their mid-60s. The oldest Boomers are preparing for retirement. They start turning 65 in 2011. The youngest Boomers are often still raising kids. Some younger Boomers are also the classic "Sandwich" generation. They feel "sandwiched" between caring for their children on the one hand and their elderly parents on the other.

Why Are the Baby Boomers Important?

1. *Size.*

    They were the biggest generation of children born in the United States. In the United States alone, 76 million babies were born during the Baby Boom, and their numbers have been supplemented by immigration. They now number over 80 million. This exceptionally large generation has always commanded the attention of the marketplace and will continue to do so for the next few

    > *This exceptionally large generation has always commanded the attention of the marketplace and will continue to do so for the next few decades.*

    decades. Because of their size, they will continue to redefine each stage of life they pass through. For example, they will become the largest market ever for products and services related to aging and retirement. They will also make new and different demands of those industries than previous generations did. The ways we market and sell these kinds of goods and services to Boomers will reshape them for future generations.

2. *Spending power.*

    It is estimated that Baby Boomers have over $2 trillion in annual spending power, a staggering figure. Simply put, they have more money to spend than any generation in human history. Boomers have spent a lifetime

    > *Simply put, they have more money to spend than any generation in human history.*

working diligently during the time of the most re-markable economic growth the world has ever known. During the recession of 2008–2009, they may have lost some of that wealth and some of their sense of affluence, but they are still the richest generation in the world. No one in marketing or selling can afford to ignore them.

3. *They buy.*

The Baby Boomers are very willing consumers. From the time they first began to accumulate some wealth in the 1980s, they have demonstrated themselves to be enthusiastic customers and clients. They are still the leading buyers of cars and other big-ticket items. Unlike their parents, whose experience of the Great Depression taught them to scrimp and save, the Boomers grew up in prosperity and affluence and learned that the best things in life can be had for the right price. They have no qualms about so-called "conspicuous consumption." They are proud of their pur-chases and see them as the reward for hard work.

> They have no qualms about so-called "conspicuous consumption."

4. *They are in transition.*

Specifically, Boomers are transitioning toward the end of their careers and retirement. As their children leave home and they retire, many will be adjusting their lifestyles, moving, buying second homes, or downsizing.

Baby Boomer Fact

The oldest Baby Boomers start turning 65 in 2011 at a rate of 10 per second.

All of these events are occasions for spending in both primary and secondary markets. Marketers and sellers who are well positioned will be able to benefit from large amounts of spending that Boomers will do as they pack their kids off to college, find new homes, search for retirement destinations, and look for a place to park their considerable investments and savings.

> *Marketers and sellers who are well positioned will be able to benefit from large amounts of spending that Boomers will do as they pack their kids off to college, find new homes, search for retirement destinations, and look for a place to park their considerable investments and savings.*

5. *They are in leadership.*

In most organizations today, you will find Baby Boomers in the leadership positions. They are the directors, the managers, the CEOs, COOs, and CFOs. When it comes to purchasing decisions, chances are it's a Boomer who has the final say. That will continue to be the case for the next decade, at least. And since Boomers are living and working longer, it will probably be longer than that. In corporate sales and business-to-business

> *In corporate sales and business-to-business marketing, Boomers are the number one market.*

Baby Boomer Fact

Fifty percent of Baby Boomers plan to buy a new home following retirement.

marketing, Boomers are the number one market. If your business depends on these kinds of transactions, appealing to them is a must.

Characteristics of Boomers

Baby Boomers: The Characteristics

Competitive

Optimistic

Idealistic

Forever young

Workaholic

Defined by their jobs

Success is visible

Avid consumers

Team players

Like face time

Like custom solutions

Nostalgic

Consult their children

Baby Boomers are 80 million strong and come in all shapes and sizes. Any description of 80 million people will contain some broad generalizations. That said, it is possible to identify some widely shared characteristics among them. Some are related to their formative experiences, and some are attributable to their life stage. While some of these characteristics may vary and evolve over time, many of them are applicable to the majority of the generation. Learning them will help you identify and relate to Boomer customers.

The Baby Boomers are:

1. *Competitive*

The Baby Boomers are a very competitive generation. This characteristic may be partly the result of the size of the generation. With so many of them around, competition for jobs, school admissions, or even the soapbox derby has always been fierce. During their lifetimes, their experience has taught them that those who compete the hardest usually win. They have carried this competitive spirit into their professional lives and it shapes them as consumers. They have perfected the art of "keeping up with the Joneses" and surpassing them. They often like to have something that's just a little bit better than what everyone else has. They revel in signs of success like awards, plaques, and trophies.

> *They often like to have something that's just a little bit better than what everyone else has.*

2. *Optimistic*

From their youth, Boomers retain the sense that things can and will keep getting better. Their experience is that if they work hard and pursue the right goals, they will be rewarded. They tend to believe the best rather than suspect the worst. If they have a plan, they believe it will work. They assume things will get better, not worse. Unlike the

> *They assume things will get better, not worse.*

younger Generation X, they are not automatically skeptical about claims and promotions. Anything is possible.

3. *Idealistic*

Boomers still carry with them some of the idealism of their youth. They believe the world *can* be a better place. They believe that, through hard work and teamwork, they can fix or improve things. Problems can be solved, solutions can be found. The best example of this was probably the 1985 "We Are the World" events, an effort by mostly Boomer musicians to end African hunger and famine through a series of fund-raising concerts. Again, anything is possible.

4. *Forever young*

Baby Boomers tend to think of themselves as 10 to 15 years younger than they really are. And they do everything they can to keep themselves young. They are more interested in physical fitness at advanced ages than previous generations—they are avid participants in fun runs and charity bike rides and are members of health clubs and gyms. They are also the target market for a multitude of drugs and treatments that fight aging and preserve youth. Many of them are planning to work beyond traditional retirement age because it helps them feel vibrant and youthful and engaged.

Baby Boomer Fact

Baby Boomers are the most likely to write their congressman or senator.

They are still a dependable market for youth-oriented products like blue jeans and red sports cars, even if they have a little trouble fitting

> *They are still a dependable market for youth-oriented products like blue jeans and red sports cars, even if they have a little trouble fitting into both these days.*

into both these days. Harley Davidson even makes a three-wheeled motorcycle for the Boomer market.

5. *Workaholics*

Boomers brought their competitive spirit and sense of commitment and hard work, giving rise to the term *workaholic*. If a full day of hard work is a recipe for success, then a longer day of hard work must be the recipe for more success. Boomers measure productivity in amount of time spent at work on the job. The more time you devote to any enterprise, they have always believed, the more successful it will be. Moreover, your work ethic should be visible for everyone to see. If it's not—if you're not visibly at work, at your desk, at the meeting, or the like—then, in their view, you're probably not working that hard.

6. *Defined by their job*

Along with Boomers' sense of competitiveness and hard work, they have come to define themselves by their jobs. Their jobs, careers, and professions form a big part of their identity—it's what they are. They revel

Baby Boomer Fact

Baby Boomers cited "work ethic" as their number one virtue in a recent Pew survey.

Baby Boomer Fact

Baby Boomers are the most loyal and committed to their employers in surveys.

in "shop talk," they attend conventions, and they make up the majority of membership in most trade and professional associations. They grew up in a time when loyalty to an employer was rewarded with tangible benefits like raises and pensions. It was also a time when membership in a career or profession conferred a certain amount of respect. Boomers are proud of what they do for a living, and they define themselves by it.

7. *Visibly successful*

Boomers believe the rewards for success should be visible and tangible. This means that they are keen on awards and recognition for accomplishments. It also means that they often seek their own rewards for success in the

> *It also means that they often seek their own rewards for success in the form of trophy purchases.*

form of trophy purchases. They have worked hard and they feel they deserve the spoils of that hard work, and they want the rewards to be visible for everyone to see and recognize.

Baby Boomer Fact

One in four Baby Boomers has a second home.

8. *Avid consumers*

Baby Boomers have always been enthusiastic consumers. Along with Baby Boomers' penchant for trophy purchases, they also grew up in a time of affluence. They grew up in families with more disposable income than at any time in history. At the same time, the range and number of consumer goods available at retail soared in postwar America.

Since they've started earning their own paychecks, they've spent more on consumer goods and services than any

> *Since they've started earning their own paychecks, they've spent more on consumer goods and services than any generation before or since.*

generation before or since. Consider this example: before the Baby Boomers, the typical person had about 15 items of clothing in his or her wardrobe; now the typical amount is 85 items. Unlike their parents' generations, Boomers are not afraid to spend their money. On the contrary, they enjoy it.

9. *Team players*

Baby Boomers like to think of themselves as part of a team. They grew up in large families, and they were surrounded by large numbers of peers through every stage of life. In their youth, sacrifice on behalf of the team was celebrated. In the 1960s, they learned the power of group action at protests and sit-ins. They are champions of teamwork in the workplace and community. They believe in strength in numbers. They feel that getting along and building relationships is the way to get things done. They

> *They would rather work with, or buy from, those who feel like part of their team.*

would rather work with, or buy from, those who feel like part of their team.

10. *People who like face time*

Baby Boomers generally like to do business face to face. They feel like that's the kind of interaction that really counts. Even though phone calls and e-mails might be more efficient, they don't offer the personal touch that Boomers' crave. Boomers are much more likely to want to meet or go to lunch to discuss business than younger generations. They view face time as "real" work time and other kinds of interactions as peripheral. They are gradually adapting to new forms of communication like social networking and texting, but don't yet feel like those kinds of exchanges are appropriate for business or sales communication.

> *Boomers are much more likely to want to meet or go to lunch to discuss business than younger generations.*

11. *Interested in custom solutions*

The Boomers were the original "Me" generation. The Boomers began the movement toward individuality. They felt there was a need for it and so they pushed for it. As a result, the Boomers are not ashamed of ego. On the contrary, they have a strong sense of individuality. They feel like they've earned the right to something special. While older generations are usually satisfied with the standard offerings that everyone else has, Boomers are happier if they feel like they have something unique. If a product or service can be tweaked a certain way so that it is one of a kind, it will likely be more attractive to

> *If a product or service can be tweaked a certain way so that it is one of a kind, it will likely be more attractive to Boomers.*

Boomers. Again, for them, success should be visible and tangible. Customizing a solution for them is like putting a monogram on their trophy purchase.

12. *Nostalgic*

Even though the 1950s and 1960s are now more than 40 years past, Baby Boomers have never really let go of them. They remember their youth fondly on every occasion. Anniversaries of events like Woodstock never pass by without a commemoration, or even a reenactment. If you turn on the radio anywhere in the country, you will find more than a few stations dedicated to the music of their youth. Movies like *American Graffiti*, *The Big Chill*, and *Stand By Me* have helped them remember and relive every stage of their lives. Nostalgia marketing aimed at Boomers is already in full swing. To attract Boomers'

> *Nostalgia marketing aimed at Boomers is already in full swing.*

attention in a recent ad, for example, the Social Security Administration used the 1960 Chubby Checker hit "The Twist," a song that touched off a dance craze of the same name in the Boomers' youth.

13. *Friends with their children*

Boomers have tended to raise their children more as their friends than as obedient subordinates. Perhaps because they were so busy with work and play, or perhaps because they were determined to raise their children differently from the way they were raised, Boomers helped create the concept of "quality time" to be spent with children. Rather then simply raising them and pushing them out the door at 18, Boomers have preferred to "get to know" their kids and do fun activities together with them, almost as peers. As their children mature into young adults, that relationship continues. Both the Boomer parents and their teen and adult Millennial children tend to advise and consult each other about big decisions and purchases.

> Both the Boomer parents and their teen and adult Millennial children tend to advise and consult each other about big decisions and purchases.

Baby Boomers are prominent and important consumers. Identifying and relating to Baby Boomer customers is not that hard—they wear their generational identities on their sleeves. And because of their prominence in our society and in the marketplace, many of us are familiar with them already. In the next chapter, we'll show you how to use your knowledge of Boomers to win them as customers and clients. It's well worth the effort. The potential rewards they offer are too significant to miss out on.

CHAPTER 3

Selling to Baby Boomers

The Search for Control

Baby Boomer Consumers

The Baby Boomers are the wealthiest generation of consumers in American history. They number over 80 million and have over $2 trillion in annual spending power. They are about a quarter of the population, but they account for over half of the spending on consumer packaged goods. Today, the Boomers are in control—they are in senior leadership and management positions at work and are at or near their earning peak. Boomers wield tremendous purchasing power in today's economy, often as the final decision makers, even when not the initial contacts.

> Today, the Boomers are in control—they are in senior leadership and management positions at work and are at or near their earning peak.

The oldest Boomers are transitioning into retirement and begin to turn 65 in 2011. The youngest Boomers are in their mid-40s, and many of them still have school-age children. Both stages usually include many occasions to spend. And, as a whole, Boomers have always been enthusiastic consumers. They are the generation that made consumption—shopping and buying—a recreational pastime. They are known for their work ethic, and they like to reward themselves for all of that hard work with the best things in life. They feel they deserve it.

The Boomers are ambitious and competitive, they like to win, and they like to be rewarded with visible signs of their success. Because there are so many of them, the Boomers are used to competing—for attention, for admission, for employment, for promotion—and they often take a competitive approach as consumers. This is the generation that wants to "keep up with the Joneses." They want to have something that's a little nicer than what everyone else has. They also like to buy products and services that are customized and unique to them. They are usually not shy about letting others know how successful they are, and conspicuous consumption is one of the ways they do that.

The Boomers are "go-getters" who believe anything is possible—or should be. As young people, they believed they could "change the world" by working together. Though many of their goals never materialized, a few did and there can be no doubt about their impact on American life. That experience instilled in the Boomers a belief that, if everyone tries their best and works hard and long, amazing things can be accomplished. They generally expect everyone they do business with, including those they are buying from, to take the same approach as they do. They don't like to take "no" for an answer or to be told that something is impossible. On the contrary, they would prefer to see evidence that you have held your nose to the grindstone and exerted maximum time and effort to make the "impossible" happen.

> *They generally expect everyone they do business with, including those they are buying from, to take the same approach as they do.*

Another legacy of the Boomers' youthful ideals is their fondness for teamwork. They have a "we're all in this together" attitude at work, and that extends to their behavior as customers. While other generations see may sales professionals as experts, facilitators, or obstacles, Boomers prefer to think of salespeople as "on their side" and part of their team. They want to have the feeling that you are all working together for a common goal.

Because of the many competing demands on their time—work, children, aging parents, workouts at the gym—Boomers often feel stressed and out of time. They will respond well to solutions that save them time and that allow them

> *They will respond well to solutions that save them time and that allow them to gain control of their surroundings.*

to gain control of their surroundings. The search for control—of their time, of their surroundings, of their finances, of their well-being, of their retirement plans, of their family's welfare—is a major motivation for the Boomer consumer. They will look for options and solutions that help them gain that control by organizing their priorities, saving time, saving money, providing efficiency, and enhancing their safety, security, and peace of mind.

One obvious means of saving time and providing efficiency is to apply technology, especially the latest forms of communication technology like e-mail, text messages, online sales and accounts, instant messaging, and social networks. If you are a member of one of the younger generations, you probably don't think twice about using technology to accomplish things quickly and easily. It's almost automatic. When you are busy and things are out of control, using the efficiency of technology is probably the first thing that comes to mind. However, members of older generations don't think the same way. Not all Baby Boomers are fully on board with the technological revolution. Some of them find new technologies confusing, some believe they are just a waste of time, and some believe they are not appropriate forms of communication for business relationships. Technology won't always seem like a solution to Baby Boomers (and Matures, of course). They might even see it as an unwelcome complication. Over the past decade, Boomers have definitely lagged behind the Millennials and Generation Xers in the adoption of the most recent innovations like smartphones and social networking. However, data from the last couple of years show that the Boomers are the fastest-growing segment of users of these same technologies. They are rapidly catching up. Thus, over the next decade or even sooner, communication technologies that are widespread among the younger generations are likely to take hold among Boomers to the same extent. All of this means that, when it comes to technology, Baby Boomers are in a period of transition and must be treated on a case-by-case basis. Some will use it, some won't, and some don't care for it at all. You have to find out which you are dealing with by asking.

Thus, over the next decade or even sooner, communication technologies that are widespread among the younger generations are likely to take hold among Boomers to the same extent.

When it comes to technology, Baby Boomers often rely on their children, mostly Millennials, to help get themselves up-to-date. In fact, Baby Boomers and their Millennial children often consult each other on a variety of purchasing and other decisions. Boomers have generally raised their children as their friends and their children are often a sounding board for them when it comes to large or important purchases. Their children's input can be very important to them, and their children will often do product research for them. By the same token, Baby Boomers will play a role in many of their children's significant purchases, especially "grown-up" purchases like homes, automobiles, insurance, and financial services. Whether the Millennial child is acting as an advisor to a Boomer who is the buyer, or vice versa, the sales professional should respect their input and advice and apply the appropriate generational tactics to each party. Sales professionals should not discount or dismiss the input of a parent or child in the sales process. The Millennial children of Boomers are an important driver of their parents' purchasing decisions, influencing an estimated \$50 billion a year of Boomer spending.

> *The Millennial children of Boomers are an important driver of their parents' purchasing decisions, influencing an estimated \$50 billion a year of Boomer spending.*

As consumers, the Baby Boomers have always offered unprecedented economic promise. Following the recession of 2008–2009, that promise dimmed a bit as Boomers suffered significant setbacks to their personal wealth. However, they remain one of the largest and wealthiest generations ever. Moreover, they continue to be avid consumers, shoppers, and buyers. Unlike younger generations, they don't mind the sales process and are open to the input of the sales professional. They are not resistant to traditional sales techniques and closing strategies the way Gen Xers and some Millennials are. In fact, because there are so many Boomers, they make up a significant number of the nation's account executives, sales professionals, and advisors. If you are a Boomer selling to other Boomers, the sales relationship will probably be a little easier to establish. You will start out with a common frame of reference and a common language, and you can build on that by appealing to your shared outlook and sense of nostalgia for your generation's experience. If you are a member of one of the younger

> *If you are a member of one of the younger generations, you will want to pay attention to the ways that the Boomer mentality differs from your own, especially in the area of communication.*

generations, you will want to pay attention to the ways that the Boomer mentality differs from your own, especially in the area of communication. But, whether you are a Boomer or not, adding some Boomer-specific tactics to your approach will give you an advantage among one of the most significant generations that the marketplace has ever seen.

Two Generations in One?

One of the unique features of the Baby Boom generation is that it is often subdivided into two subgenerations, Early or Leading Edge Boomers (b. 1946–1954) and Late Boomers, also known as Generation Jones (b. 1955–1964). Although these two subgroups share many of the same formative experiences and attitudes, they are at different life stages and may have different spending priorities. The oldest of the Early Boomers begin to reach traditional retirement age in 2011. For the most part, their children are adults and they are focused on concluding their careers, transitioning to retired life, and securing their children's and their own futures. Many of them are grandparents. Many will be moving to new homes, shifting their assets to more conservative investments, downsizing and simplifying their lifestyles, and focusing on preserving their health and longevity.

However, the youngest members of Generation Jones often still have children in school and are in mid-career.

Do: Try to discern whether your Boomer clients fit into the "Late" or "Early" categories of Baby Boomers.

Don't: Assume that the oldest Boomers and youngest Boomers will have exactly the same outlook and needs.

Because the retirement age will increase over the next few decades, they may be as many as 25 years away from retirement. They will have different priorities such as getting their kids through school and off to college, improving and upgrading their homes and lifestyles, and building their personal wealth. The distinction between these generations is especially important for sales professionals in the fields of financial services and retirement planning, and also for those who deal in products and services that are considered major, "life" purchases like real estate, automobiles, education, and mortgages. Sales and account executives and advisors will want to discern which end of the Baby Boomer spectrum they are dealing with before deciding which products and features to emphasize.

Some observers have also noted a more subtle difference between the older and younger groups of Baby Boomers, a difference in outlook or mind-set. For the most part, Early and Late Boomers seem to share the qualities of ambition and competitiveness and both seem to be enthusiastic consumers. However,

> *Leading Edge Boomers tend to be more typically Boomer-like in their attitudes, while members of Generation Jones seem to have a tinge of the skepticism that we usually associate with Generation X.*

Leading Edge Boomers tend to be more typically Boomer-like in their attitudes, while members of Generation Jones seem to have a tinge of the skepticism that we usually associate with Generation X. This makes sense when you consider the proximity in age of the youngest members of Generation Jones to older members of Generation X.

Early Boomers have reason to remain a little more idealistic and optimistic than Late Boomers. The "system" that they've worked in and paid into will still be there to repay them. They have taken some financial hits from the recession of 2008–2009 but, for the most part, their investments have grown with the country's prosperity and will be there to reward them. They still have reason to pursue the dreams they have always looked forward to. Sales professionals can be part of the team that makes those dreams come true. Late Boomers, however, had less time to accumulate wealth before the economic setbacks. They have felt the pain of the economic downturns more sharply. They may be less optimistic and more pragmatic. For them, the "dream" has been diminished and postponed. They probably prefer to know the cold, hard facts and to try and find the best-case scenario. Sales professionals can help them by working with them to find the best possible solutions to fit their new realities.

When working with customers who are on the borderline between generations, the smartest approach is figure out which generational characteristics they exhibit most and then choose the appropriate tactics.

When surveyed, many Late Boomers do not classify themselves as Baby Boomers. They may be more skeptical of sales pitches and ad campaigns and require more of the straightforward and informative approach preferred by Gen Xers. This also underscores the idea that, when choosing generational sales tactics, it's more important to figure out the generational mind-set of your customers rather than focusing on exact birth date. When working with customers who are on the borderline between generations, the smartest approach is figure out which generational characteristics they exhibit most and then choose the appropriate tactics.

Identifying and Understanding Your Baby Boomer Customers

To find out if Baby Boomers are potential or actual customers for you, utilize some of the simple market research techniques spelled out in Chapter 1. If you have existing documentation with your customers' ages or dates of birth, you can simply analyze and categorize it. If you want to gather the data from your Boomer customers, do not rely exclusively on means that are heavy on technology, like e-mail and social networking. You will miss some of your older customers, at least at this point in time. Methods that involve discounts or promotions should appeal to them. If you'd like to know if Boomers are generally interested in your products and services, or have the potential to be, you can use the Internet and association resources discussed in the first chapter.

Identifying Boomer customers who are right in front of you might be harder than it seems, at least from visual clues. Boomers who are in their 60s might be confused with Matures. It's important to remember that even the oldest Boomers were in their teens and 20s in the 1960s and often have a strong and distinct generational identity. They might be retirees now, but they may still think of themselves as the

To Do

Use the basic market research techniques suggested in Chapter 1 to learn about your Baby Boomer customers and potential customers. Don't exclusively use e-mail, online, and instant messaging techniques—you will miss some Boomers that way.

flower children they were 40 years ago. On the other end of the spectrum, Boomers who are in their 40s, members of Generation Jones, may be very young in appearance and have young children, leading you to think of them as members of Generation X. As we mentioned earlier, that impulse may lead you in the right direction, an approach that blends both Boomer and Gen X tactics.

Identifying and Understanding Your Baby Boomer Customers

Feel, look, and act younger than they are

Enjoy conspicuous consumption

Supermoms (and superdads) who do it all

Like to talk face to face

Of two minds on technology

Show visible emotion

Display visible signs of success

Like common courtesies

Here are some clues to the Baby Boomer mind-set that will help you recognize Boomers when you are doing business with them:

- *Forever young.* Although they may be grandparents in their 60s, most Baby Boomers have no intention of giving in to old age. Most Baby Boomers of any age like to cultivate a youthful appearance and attitude. Their favorite consumer brands are still Levis and Harley Davidson. They like to stay fit and keep their hair from going gray or going away. This is not to say that they dress and present themselves the way that today's younger generations do. But neither have they adopted the appearance that their parents' generation did at the same age. They like to think of themselves as 15 years younger than they really are, and they like to look that way, too.

- *Conspicuous consumption.* Beginning with their days as the Yuppies of the 1980s, Boomers have always liked to reward themselves with the finer things in life. They view luxuries as rewards for hard work and trophies for their accomplishment. They are looking for the best of the best—name brands, designer labels, and high-end goods. Expensive cars, clothes, electronics, and appliances are the visible signs of their success. These are the lifestyle elements—a BMW, a designer kitchen, a Ralph Lauren jacket—that let everyone know that they have made it. The recent recession may have compromised their dreams and their free spending a little, but this basic impulse is still there.

- *Supermoms and superdads.* They do it all. They work long hours, and they chauffeur the kids to school, soccer, and play dates and spend "quality time" with them when they're not driving them around. They remodel the kitchen, landscape the yard, and plant a garden. They manage their investments and their finances. They shop for themselves and their families. They take the pets to the vet and the clothes to the cleaners. They revel in how much they can do in one day. But because they are busy and stressed, they are always looking for ways to save time and get control of their surroundings.

> *If a product or service, or even the sales process itself, can save them some work and time, they will be interested.*

If a product or service, or even the sales process itself, can save them some work and time, they will be interested.

- *Like to talk.* Baby boomers like face time and talking on the phone. Those are their preferred methods of communication. They usually do not shy away from small talk or sales talk. For Boomers, face-to-face or person-to-person communication is the way things get done in the business world.

> *For Boomers, face-to-face or person-to-person communication is the way things get done in the business world.*

If you spend time talking with them, you will get credit for your time and effort. It is proof that you are working hard for them.

- *Lower-tech.* Although Baby Boomers are gradually adopting smartphones and other high-tech gizmos, they do not brandish them as fashion accessories or use them to demonstrate how cool they are. Likewise, they are not likely to be impressed by how tech-savvy you are. On the contrary, some Boomers are intimidated by high-tech communication, finding it overly complicated and difficult to learn. Others see high-tech gadgets as toys that young people use to waste huge amounts of time. Again, this is one feature of Boomers that may change over the next several years as they increasingly adopt the technologies that everyone else uses. However, it's unlikely that they will come to see technology use as part of their identity in the way that younger generations do.

- *Visible emotion.* Boomers are more likely to be more expressive about their emotions—whether it's delight or disappointment—than other generations. Matures tend to be more reserved, while the younger generations tend to be more guarded, aloof, or expressionless. Boomers, however, learned in their heyday that it was OK to express emotions and "let it all hang out." Many Boomers freely communicate their optimism and their can-do spirits. They will often let you know with a facial or verbal expression whether they are pleased or not.

- *Wall of fame.* Boomers believe that success should be visible. They revel in outward and tangible signs of their accomplish-ments. If you visit a Boomer client in his or her home or office

> *They revel in outward and tangible signs of their accomplishments.*

and see a shelf of trophies or a wall full of plaques and certificates of achievement, you are likely working with someone that has the Boomer mind-set.

- *Like courtesy.* Boomers still prefer the common courtesies of old, like formal introductions, saying "please" and "thank you," dressing appropriately for the setting, and formal titles like Mr., Ms., and Dr. They don't necessarily want you to be deferential, but they don't want you to be overly casual and familiar. They see these courtesies

> They see these courtesies as important signs of respect and not outdated niceties.

as important signs of respect and not outdated niceties. Likewise, Boomers prefer to speak and communicate in complete sentences and not in slang or popular expressions. They may be taken aback if someone whom they don't know well uses an overly informal manner or slang and off-color language.

Using these clues, along with what you know about their characteristics from the Baby Boomer snapshot, you should be able to recognize and understand customers that have the Baby Boomer outlook. Once you know you're working with a Baby Boomer, you can select the appropriate approach.

Engaging Your Baby Boomer Customers

Earning likability and respect from Baby Boomers is a matter of appealing to their generational personality. Getting Baby Boomers to listen and "lean forward" may be easier than with other generations. They are open-minded, optimistic, and enthusiastic consumers who respond well to many traditional sales techniques. Adding these Boomer-specific tactics will give you an extra advantage when selling to this large and wealthy generation.

- *Optimism.* The Boomers tend to be optimists. They are largely upbeat and prefer optimistic and upbeat people, even more than most. Get your smiles and your optimism

Engaging Your Baby Boomer Customers

Show optimism.

Feature brand names.

Use person-to-person communication.

Help them get control of their time and surroundings.

Provide a sense of teamwork.

Offer customized solutions.

Don't make them feel old.

Don't be afraid to sell.

tuned up for your Boomer meetings. A cheerful demeanor will make more of an impression on Boomers than it will on younger generations. Conversely, a dry and emotionless presentation will bother Boomers more than it will

> *A cheerful demeanor will make more of an impression on Boomers than it will on younger generations.*

Millennials and Xers. Perhaps you have some good news to share, something positive that's going on in your business or industry. Emphasize the ways that your

To Do

Find some positive or upbeat news about your business or industry to share with Boomer clients.

products or services can provide positive experiences for them. Be upbeat and optimistic, especially with the older Early Boomers.

- *Brand names.* Boomers are pretty loyal to brand names that they've heard of and used. While younger generations might be willing to switch to the new start-up company based on price and novelty, Boomers will be more inclined to stick with

> Boomers will be more inclined to stick with what they know and trust.

what they know and trust. If what you're selling is a major brand, or backed by a major brand, Boomers will be more likely to be interested. If what you're selling is new and not well known, you'll need to give them some good reasons to consider it.

- *Communication.* Boomers like to communicate the old-fashioned way—by talking face to face or on the phone. They prefer fully formed sentences and presentations to a casual and disorganized talk. Think about what you will say or write before you start. When writing to Baby Boomers, use the appropriate format for business communications and address them personally. Boomers

---

Do: Communicate with Boomers using standard business communication and organized presentations.

Don't: Start a relationship with a Boomer by using an overly casual manner or language.

To Do

Before you meet or speak with Boomer clients, think about and organize what you are going to say so that it gives the impression of competence and professionalism.

respect professionalism in the workplace, and that carries over into the marketplace. When they are doing business with you, they expect you to communicate as they would in their own businesses. When moving from one step

> *When they are doing business with you, they expect you to communicate as they would in their own businesses.*

to another in the sales process, explain to them what you are doing. This will help establish your competence and work ethic with Boomers.

- *Efficiency.* If your products or services have some time-saving elements or can help them gain control of their busy lives, Boomers will be interested. When selling to Boomers, emphasize these features early in the sales pro-

> *Let them know that what you are selling and the way you do business will make their lives less complicated.*

  cess. Let them know that what you are selling and the way you do business will make their lives less complicated. Highlight products, services, or features that "will do the work for you."

- *Teamwork.* When preparing to meet with a Boomer prospect, remember that they value teamwork. You are there to determine how your product and service can add value to their lives. When selling a product or service, mention the people behind it and explain their role on the team, just as Boomers are part of the larger team. You are not a vendor or an agent, you are a teammate.

> You are not a vendor or an agent, you are a teammate.

Consider saying something like: "I appreciate your business and the opportunity to be part of your team. Let's tackle this together and see if we can find the best solution."

- *Customize.* The original "Me" generation has a bit of ego to address, so if you are able to offer customization to fit their exact needs, you will have an edge. Do not enter the conversation assuming you already understand their needs—ask. Let them know that you can provide a solution that is unique to their needs. Then customize your solution to meet their needs.

> Let them know that you can provide a solution that is unique to their needs.

Subtly emphasize that you recognize their uniqueness. Don't make a fuss over it; just let them know that you are aware of it.

- *Still young.* Boomers think of themselves as at least 15 years younger than they really are. Speak and sell to them the way they think of themselves. Assume that they think of themselves as fit and active. Avoid terms such as *active adult, mature, older adult, 50-plus,* and even *middle-aged*—the Boomers understand what these code words mean. Don't describe something as "right for someone your age." Boomers will hear that as "right for an old person like you."

> **Do:** Assume that even older Boomers think of themselves as young, fit, and active.
>
> **Don't:** Make reference to their actual age, even in a coded or subtle way, or describe your offering as "right for your age."

- *Sell.* The Boomers are not adverse to sales and advertising. They understand that sales and marketing are essential to successful businesses and see them as perfectly honorable professions. They are accustomed to and comfortable with traditional sales techniques and approaches. The Boomers and Matures will give you the opportunity to sell in the way that you have learned to. Find out what their needs and wants are. Put your products' best features forward and don't forget the bells and whistles. Ask for their business. Ask to move to the next step. Along the same lines, so-called vanity advertising that includes a photo of you and trumpets your accomplishments and credentials does not work with younger generations, but is good for reminding Boomers who you are and establishing your credibility with them.

> *The Boomers and Matures will give you the opportunity to sell in the way that you have learned to.*

Building Sales Relationships with Baby Boomer Customers

Once you've engaged Baby Boomers and gotten them to lean forward and listen to you, the next step is to build a

Building Sales Relationships with Baby Boomer Customers

Show them you're working hard for them.

Court them.

Offer some visible signs of accomplishment.

Find their comfort level with technology.

Respect and incorporate their children's input.

Appeal to their sense of ego.

Help them feel visionary.

Appeal to their sense of nostalgia.

relationship with them, to ensure that you are "part of their team." Some sales take a few minutes, while others can take weeks or even months. In any case, there are some easy ways to build your relationships with Boomer consumers. Baby Boomers are typically very loyal to brands and people. Once you establish yourself as a trusted source, Boomers are not likely to go elsewhere. Here are some suggestions for building sales relationships with Baby Boomers:

- *Show your work.* Boomers are known for their work ethic, and they want to see that same quality when they are doing business with you. Show them that you are putting in the time on their account.

  > *Call them or meet with them in person to remind them that you are on the case.*

  Call them or meet with them in person to remind them that you are on the case. Explain all that you have done for them with your calls, paperwork, meetings, and negotiations. Demonstrate your willingness to compete for their business by going the extra mile.

- *Court them.* Invest in relationships with Boomers. Satisfy their need for face time with lunches, dinners, outings, meetings, or excursions. Make sure they understand that their business is important to you. Send cards or letters at appropriate times. Call them personally to let them know about special promotions and offers.

> *Make sure they understand that their business is important to you.*

- *Trophies.* The Boomers are competitive, like to win, and like to be rewarded for it with visible signs of their success. Offer Boomers rewards for doing business with you. Is there a thank-you gift that they can subtly display in their office or home? A nice pen? Paperweight? Golf shirt? Let Boomers know that you recognize their contribution to your business and then give them a way to remember and display that contribution as an achievement.

- *Appropriate technology.* Do not assume that Baby Boomers can use all the forms of communication that you use. Do not assume that they cannot. Baby Boomers are adopting technology at an accelerating pace. Still, many of them are not comfortable with it. You must ask Boomers specifically what kinds of communication they prefer.

To Do

Have some giveaways or rewards to give your Boomer clients as visible signs of accomplishment.

Then honor their preferences. Many Boomers have become adept at technology, but most still value the hu-

> *Many Boomers have become adept at technology, but most still value the human touch.*

man touch. Even if a Boomer is comfortable with e-mail and other kinds of messaging, you will still want to supplement that with good old-fashioned notes, letters, cards, and phone calls from time to time, unless your customer specifically prefers you not to.

- *Baby on board.* Remember the "Baby on Board" signs that used to hang in the windows of family cars? Those were proud and doting Boomer parents driving those cars with their Millennial children safely secured in car seats in the back. Boomer parents usually still have their kids in tow, even if the children are adults. They tend to stay in regular contact, talking several times a day. The Boomers are influenced by their children's input, and their children will often do product research

  > *Be prepared for their children to be influential in some way in the sales process.*

  for them. Be prepared for their children to be influential in some way in the sales process. Be respectful of the children's presence and input.

Do: Ask your Boomer customers which forms of communication they prefer to use.

Don't: Assume your Boomer customers are comfortable with all the forms of technology that you use. And don't assume they aren't, either.

Do: Be respectful of the influence of Boomers' children on their purchasing decisions.

Don't: Dismiss or discount children's input, even if it is not helpful to you.

Utilize some Millennial selling approaches to connect with Boomers' children. You can even preempt the children's research efforts by giving them some online resources as a place to start looking. Do not discount or dismiss the children's opinions. Their Boomer parents certainly won't.

- *Flatter and praise.* The Boomers are proud of their work ethic and their accomplishments. Let them know that you recognize and appreciate what they have done. Tell them that they deserve to be rewarded.

  Help them feel victorious.

  Help them feel victorious. Consider saying something like: "You've worked hard. You've accomplished more than most. You deserve the best. Let's make sure you get it."

- *Vision.* The Boomers think big. As flower children in the 1960s, they set out to "change the world." As Yuppies in the 1980s, they sang along with "We are the world, we are the children" to help end hunger. They like to feel like what they are doing is groundbreaking and important. Help give them the sense that they are building and working toward something big and that their decisions fit into a vision for a better and brighter future.

- *Nostalgia.* The Boomers are definitely nostalgic for the highlights of their generational experiences. They like to be reminded and to reminisce about being a kid in the 1950s and a young person in the 1960s and 1970s. The music, movies, and movements of those times exert a strong emotional pull on them. This can be difficult to insert into a sales relationship unless your products or services have a direct appeal to their sense of nostalgia or unless you are a Boomer yourself and can share memories with them. Still, if the subject comes up, it won't hurt to indulge Boomer clients in a walk down memory lane.

The Last Look: Closing the Deal with Baby Boomers

Closing the deal with Baby Boomers can be simple and straightforward: ask for their business. While consumers of all generations are increasingly resistant to high-pressure sales techniques and scare tactics, Baby Boomers (and Matures, for that matter) are still open to traditional sales and closing strategies. They want to know about the "sizzle" as well as the steak, and they will usually give you the time and attention to make your case, to show in your words and actions that you are genuinely interested in their business. To get to the "yes" with Boomers, you must appeal sincerely to their sense of ego and work ethic and then flat out ask for the sale.

To Do

Demonstrate to Boomers that you are working hard for their business and then ask for the sale.

Once you have made a connection with Boomers, established yourself as competent and knowledgeable, and demonstrated that you understand their needs, you can offer them a solution that you have devised to match what they want. Then you can ask to move to the next step. As you move through each step, let them know what you are doing. Follow through with them, and follow up to let them know that you are still working for them and that you want the sale. Once you show them that you have the

> *Once you show them that you have the ability to deliver what they want, they probably won't shop around elsewhere.*

ability to deliver what they want, they probably won't shop around elsewhere.

Baby Boomers offer opportunities to cultivate long-lasting sales relationships. As a generation, they offer more in potential sales than any other. They are a large and wealthy generation and they enjoy being consumers. They will give you the chance to do what you do

> *They will give you the chance to do what you do best, and they will reward you for it.*

best, and they will reward you for it. By applying a little generational insight in your dealings with Boomer customers, your results from this important sector can be that much better.

For Further Thought on Your Boomer Customers

1. Is your product or service ready for the Boomer transition into retirement? Is it something that they consume only during their peak earning years? If it is, how do you begin to establish the value of your

product or service as the Boomers move into the next stage of their life? How do you transition with them?

2. In business-to-business relationships, have you met the person who will replace your Baby Boomer buyer when he or she retires? Have you begun establishing a relationship with him or her? Are they a different generation? If so, which? And how will you change how you interact with this new person to keep your relationship strong?

3. Are there accounts where the transition from one buyer of one generation to a new buyer in a different generation represents an opportunity for you to do business with new customers?

4. Consider your own Baby Boomer sales agents—are they transferring information on their customers to their replacement so that when they retire, this valuable customer information is not lost.

5. Is there any part of your store, shop, or buying environment that may cause your Boomer customers to have to ask embarrassing questions due to technology or other things that are assumed to be common knowledge by the younger generations? How can you solve this? No one, regardless of his or her generation, likes the feeling of embarrassment.

Takeaways

Consumers from the Baby Boom generation will buy products and services:

- That appeal to their sense of youth, accomplishment, and ego

- From sales professionals who are part of their "team"
- That are customized for them
- That remind them of their generational experience or are nostalgic
- From salespeople who appear professional, competent, and courteous
- That help them gain control of their time and surroundings
- From sales professionals who work hard and ask for their business
- When they are rewarded for their success or patronage
- From salespeople who convey a sense of optimism
- From sales professionals who put in the time and face time to match their own work ethic

Snapshot of Millennials

Meet the Millennials

Millennials were born between 1980 and 2000 into a world ubiquitous with technology. As of the most recent census figures, Millennials have become the largest generation in the United States, at 85 million strong. For the majority of their lives, they only saw a growing economy. The recession of 2008–2009 was the first major change in the country's economic pace that they experienced. They are the children of the Baby Boomers and the oldest Gen Xers, and they have grown up protected, praised, and programmed by their parents. However, they grew up with threats to their security that would be new to older generations, such as terrorism and school shootings.

> They are the children of the Baby Boomers and the oldest Gen Xers, and they have grown up protected, praised, and programmed by their parents.

Millennials may be the most important demographic in the marketplace today—and the most misunderstood. They are teens and 20-somethings, but they already seem to have a sense of entitlement. They often appear too casual or in too much of a hurry. They might say they want to change the world but spend most of their time sending text messages or checking their Facebook pages. They express their individuality with quirky clothes, music, and tattoos but never want to go anywhere without their friends. They proudly proclaim their independence but seem content to live at home well into adulthood. Parents and professionals alike might be

Millennial Fact

Over 40 percent of Millennials have a tattoo. Twenty percent have more than one.

tempted to throw their hands up and mutter a favorite Millennial expression, "Whatever!"

However, because of their size and spending power, misunderstanding Millennials is not a mistake that any sales professional can afford to make. The Millennial generation is already reshaping the marketplace and will continue to do so for years to come. This chapter offers a snapshot of the Millennial generation. You can use this chapter as a sort of "field guide" to identify and recognize Millennials by their characteristics and their behavior in the marketplace and to track Millennials going forward, as they mature and evolve as consumers.

Who Are the Millennials?

Who are the Millennials, and why is everyone talking about them? Simply put, the Millennials are the largest generation

Millennials: The Demographics

Born: 1980–2000
Population: Nearly 85 million
Spending power: $1.5 trillion
Most diverse generation in U.S. history
Most educated generation in U.S. history

since the Baby Boomers and will ultimately be the most influential and biggest-spending generation in history. They were born in the last two decades of the twentieth century between 1980 and 2000, and they now number about 85 million. They are already the most educated, tech-savvy, and diverse generation we have known. Among them are the founders and CEOs of companies like Facebook and YouTube, entrepreneurs who are reshaping technology and commerce, and the entertainers and athletes who are presiding over popular culture at the box office, on television, in music, and on the Internet.

> *They are already the most educated, tech-savvy, and diverse generation we have known.*

For all their promise and potential, though, Millennials can seem a confounding and frustrating bunch to those in older generations who live and work with them, especially if your success depends on understanding, marketing, and selling to them. They have a reputation as "Generation Me" for their apparent sense of entitlement. They can appear unmotivated or unengaged, overly dependent on both technology and their parents. They sport tattoos and piercings in much larger numbers than previous generations and are most comfortable when wearing flip-flops and sending a text message, both of which they'll do just about anywhere. On the one hand, they seem to have a moral obligation to recycle a can or a bottle but, on the other, have no problem downloading or copying a movie or a song, illegally, as long as it is free. Trends

> *On the one hand, they seem to have a moral obligation to recycle a can or a bottle but, on the other, have no problem downloading or copying a movie or a song, illegally, as long as it is free.*

What's In A Name?

Millennials are called that because they are coming of age in a new millennium. Also known as: Generation Y, the Echo Boom, Generation Next, and Generation Net.

gain instant favor with them, known as "going viral," and that favor is just as instantly lost.

Why Are They Called "Millennials"?

In 1991, noted generational experts William Strauss and Neil Howe coined the term *Millennials* in their landmark book *Generations*, and defined the generation as those born between 1982 and 2001, who would come of age in a new millennium. Later, the term *Generation Y* was applied by the influential magazine *Advertising Age* in 1993 to those born in the late 1970s to differentiate them from the preceding Generation X for advertisers and marketers. Around the same time, demographers who study population trends began to use the terms *Echo Boom* and *Echo Generation* to refer to the surge in the number of births in the United States between the early 1980s and the mid-1990s. Because these were largely the children of Baby Boomers, they were regarded as an "echo" of that population boom. To make maters even more confusing, PBS and a few other organizations use the term *Generation Next*. Today, you will find these terms, *Millennial*, *Generation Y*, *Generation Next*, and *Echo Boomers*, used interchangeably. For purposes of clarity, we will stick to the term *Millennials*. It has become the most common and, when surveyed, Millennials say that's the name they prefer for their generation, but studies and surveys that use the other terms are really talking about the same generation.

When Were They Born?

Short answer: 1980–2000. As with the generation's name, you will find a variety of starting and ending dates offered by experts and demographers as the parameters of the Millennial generation. Some say it began as early as 1974, others as late as 1983. Some say it ended with the decline in births after 1994; others include those born as late as 2004. For dates, we will use the easy-to-remember parameters of 1980–2000. Those dates fall within or near the estimates of most experts. Thus, in 2010, Millennial were roughly between the ages of 10 and 30. That said, as with all generational labels, it is important to remember that someone born in 1999 will likely have more in common with someone born in 2001 than someone born in 1981. By the same token, a person born in the early 1980s is currently at a different life stage (early career) than someone born in the late 1990s (teen years). Though we use a rough age range to define Millennials, the key points are:

- Shared experiences, characteristics, and tendencies will be more important in identifying Millennials than exact birth date.
- Today, Millennials are teenagers and 20-somethings; they comprise the entire youth market, a key demographic group for anyone in sales and marketing.

You may see studies and surveys that refer to the generation with different names and varying dates. Don't be confused. Just remember that we are all talking about the same thing: a generation usually known as the "Millennials" who were born roughly between 1980 and 2000 and who are now in their teens and 20s.

Formative Experiences

Millennials were born and grew up in times of economic growth and prosperity. The Great Recession of 2008 was their first real experience of economic hard times. Their youth has also witnessed explosive growth in technology, particularly in the expansion of the Internet and the World

---

Millennials: The Formative Experiences

Economic prosperity of the 1990s

Revolution in technology

Columbine and other school shootings

Parents as friends

Parents as drivers to multiple scheduled activities

September 11, 2001

Iraq and Afghanistan

Monica Lewinsky and the impeachment

Hanging chads

The Great Recession

MySpace, Facebook, YouTube, and Twitter

Wide Web and in mobile technology, especially text messaging. Their childhoods were typically very planned, programmed, scheduled, and carefully managed by their parents, often well into their postadolescence. Remember all the talk about soccer moms? These are the kids they raised.

Their sense of threat and insecurity comes from sources unique to their generation's youth, such as school shootings like Columbine and terrorist attacks like 9/11. They grew up watching multiple television channels, like Nickelodeon, devoted to children, as well as books and movies designed for them, like *Harry Potter*. They have been accustomed to waves of media and marketing aimed right at them, most of which they don't find either bothersome or effective. They've always had 200+ channels of TV and don't find any of them particularly compelling. As adolescents and college students, they literally

> *They have been accustomed to waves of media and marketing aimed right at them, most of which they don't find either bothersome or effective.*

Millennials: The Life Stage

Millennials are in their teens and 20s. Adult Millennials often seem stuck in a stage between adolescence and adulthood—adult-olescence, if you will. They are in college and in their early careers. Almost half still live at home. They generally defer marriage, childbearing, and career decisions until later than previous generations. The oldest Millennials are beginning to start families and buy homes. The average first-time homebuyer is a Millennial.

invented social media, now the most popular category of online activity among all generations.

Why Are the Millennials Important?

They Are the Youth Market

As mentioned earlier, Millennials now comprise the entire youth market. For most products and services, the youth market is a critically important demographic, often the most important, for a number of reasons. First, young people have disproportionate spending power—most of their income is disposable. They also wield tremendous influence on the spending of others. Beyond that, they influence consumer culture in general by conferring "buzz" or "cool" on certain products. Products that become popular among young people generally go on to enjoy success in the wider market. Young people wield even greater influence over the spending of their parents and family, who give them access to a much larger pool of spending power. This is especially true of Millennials, who often remain dependent on their parents until well into their 20s. Finally, cultivating the youth market also offers the potential for creating long-term brand loyalty among consumers who will be active in the marketplace for years to come.

> *Products that become popular among young people generally go on to enjoy success in the wider market.*

Size

After age, the most important feature of the Millennial generation is its *size*. Simply put, the Millennial generation

is now the largest generation in American history.
Why is their size impor-
tant? As we learned from
the Baby Boomers, when

> *Simply put, the Millennial generation is now the largest generation in American history.*

an exceptionally large generation makes its way through
life's stages, it has the power to reshape ideas about education,
careers, and family, as well as commerce, marketing, and sales.
Just as Baby Boomers created and drove new, youth-oriented
markets for popular culture and fashion, the Millennials are
creating and driving new markets, such as those in personal
communication, networking, and technology.

Furthermore, big generations like the Boomers and
the Millennials have the power to reshape aspects of society
and culture. Therefore, they will not only create and drive
markets for new products and services, but also reshape how
all products and services, new or traditional, are bought
and sold. Because they
combine the cultural and
consumer influence of
a very large generation
with the already powerful
cultural and consumer
influence of youth, Mil-
lennials are poised to
dominate the market-
place, just as the Boomers
did in their youth. In other

> *Because they combine the cultural and consumer influence of a very large generation with the already powerful cultural and consumer influence of youth, Millennials are poised to dominate the marketplace, just as the Boomers did in their youth.*

words, the way we market and sell to Millennials will become
the way we do business in general. Indeed, we have already seen
the impact of this influence in important consumer fields such
as personal technology, telecommunication, social media, and
social networking.

Millennial Fact

Millennials have recently overtaken Baby Boomers as the largest generation in the United States.

Spending Power

Millennials are also important because of their considerable spending power. Millennials wield about $1.5 trillion in annual spending power. When spending on housing is removed from the equation, they have already surpassed Generation X in annual spending. This is especially impressive when you consider that half of Millennials are still teenagers and the other half are in college or in their lowest earning years. Compare that to Generation X, which is approaching its peak earning years but is not able to keep up in spending with Millennials. Millennials are surpassing Gen Xers in spending partly because of their size, and partly because they have access to the spending power of their mostly Baby Boomer parents. Baby Boomers spend over $2 *trillion* annually. Millennials are thought to directly influence approximately $50 to $100 billion of Boomer spending, in addition to what they spend themselves. What's more, just as Millennials have overtaken Boomers in population size, they will also eventually outstrip Boomers in annual spending as they approach their own peak earning years. Put it all together and you have the

> *Millennials wield about $1.5 trillion in annual spending power.*

> *Millennials are thought to directly influence approximately $50 to $100 billion of Boomer spending, in addition to what they spend themselves.*

Millennial Facts

Over 90 percent of Millennials use text messaging and social media. One-third of Millennials average 100 text messages a day. Eighty-three percent of Millennials sleep with their cell phones.

biggest-spending youth market in history that will one day become the biggest-spending generation in history.

Technology

In addition to their age, size, and spending power, Millennials are an important sector of the market because of their dominance of the technology marketplace. That means two things:

1. Millennials are among the leading purchasers of high-tech devices like smartphones, netbooks, and tablet computers.
2. Millennials are the leading users of social networking, social media, and other venues in the online marketplace.

Thus, this generation is shaping both the hardware and the software of Internet commerce, influencing not only what we buy but also how we buy it. Through their pioneering use of music-sharing sites like Napster, online retailers like Amazon and iTunes, and social networking and media sites like Facebook and YouTube, Millennials have been the architects of the connected marketplace.

> ## Millennial Fact
>
> Seventy percent of Millennials have downloaded "pirated" copies of music and/or movies.

They have, in effect, created new real estate for marketing and sales. For them, these new electronic storefronts and billboards have become every bit as important as traditional brick-and-mortar stores. And the norm for transactions in this new "virtual" retail space—fast, easy, connected, and inexpensive—has become the expected standard for any retail space, including brick-and-mortar stores.

Buzz

Millennials create what the ad industry calls "social currency," which, simply put, is what makes certain companies "cool," gives certain products "buzz," or makes ideas go "viral." And Millennials are the arbiters of what has buzz and what goes viral today. Social currency is gained by linking your products and services with qualities, ideas, and images that generate positive feelings among target consumers and encourages them to advocate for your business in their social environments. It can be measured with metrics like number of Twitter followers, Facebook fans,

> *Social currency is gained by linking your products and services with qualities, ideas, and images that generate positive feelings among target consumers and encourages them to advocate for your business in their social environments.*

or YouTube hits, and in other ways. Some generators of social currency are environmental or "green" practices; an emphasis on technology; the use of sleek, minimalist design; quirky individuality; affordability; and simplicity, among others. Of course, your business does not have to be an environmental, technology, or design firm to take advantage of the social currency generated by those concepts. Rather, your business simply has to find ways to attach itself to those concepts in the marketing and selling processes.

Although the idea of social currency has always been part of marketing and selling, it has become particularly important among Millennials for a couple of reasons:

1. Because of their interconnectedness, through text messaging, social networking, and other media, Millennials can relay social currency to one another, literally at light speed. They dominate the technologies of telecommunication and social networking, and those are now the primary means of "going viral" or generating "buzz."

2. Millennials are the natural trendsetters today because of their age and the size of their generation. Millennials will set the definition for the "cool factor," and the marketplace at large will follow.

Any generalizations about a group of 85 million people must be overbroad and will include many exceptions. Nonetheless, in surveys and studies, certain characteristics are consistently associated with the Millennial generation. Generations typically acquire shared characteristics because they share formative experiences. Some characteristics may evolve over time as a generation moves through different life stages or as times change. The following are characteristics

Millennials: The Characteristics

Diverse

Educated

Adult-olescent

Love technology

Issue and cause oriented

Peer oriented

Individual identities

In a hurry

Optimistic

Ambitious but directionless

Busy and stressed

Raised as parents' friends

Well cared for and programmed

associated with Millennials and how they might affect their behavior as consumers:

1. *They are diverse.*

One important characteristic of Millennials is that they are the most diverse generation, by race and ethnicity, in American history. Racial and ethnic minorities make up almost 40 percent of the Millennial generation, compared to 20 percent of the Matures and 27 percent of the Boomers. In addition, Millennials have grown up with an awareness of the diversity of their peers and have been taught to value tolerance and diversity. They hold tolerance as a moral value, more so than other generations, and expect that

> *Your Millennial clients are more likely to come from ethnic minorities and likely to find the values of tolerance and diversity appealing.*

others will, too. Your Millennial clients are more likely to come from ethnic minorities and likely to find the values of tolerance and diversity appealing.

2. *They are educated.*

Millennials are well on their way to becoming the most educated generation in America. They graduate from high school and attend college at rates that surpass all previous generations. Theirs will be the first generation in which a majority has some college education. This re-

> *Theirs will be the first generation in which a majority has some college education.*

flects the rise of the social and economic value of education as well as Millennials' tendency to delay starting their careers. It means that your Millennial customers will consider themselves smart and savvy consumers, able to research and read about products independent of sales advice. They will appreciate access to resources for detailed research and comparison.

3. *They are "adult-olescent."*

Millennials are delaying marriage and childbearing until later ages than any previous generation. Again, this is part of a larger pattern of this generation's delaying the traditional markers of adulthood until their mid-20s. Only 25 percent of adult (ages 19–30) Millennials are now married; only 12 percent

Millennial Fact

Forty-seven percent of adult Millennials still live with their families.

are married with children. Conversely, 47 percent of adult Millennials continue to live with their parents or other family members. Even if they don't live with their parents, they often rely on the advice and input of their parents regarding their education, careers, and major purchases. They value their parents and think of them as friends. They are also more likely to cohabitate without marrying than previous generations. This means that your Millennial customers may not exhibit the signs of independent adulthood—family, career, and homeownership—until they are in their late 20s. Their income is thus more disposable and more likely to be concentrated on items for personal use, like electronics, music, and fashion, than on products and services for homes and family members.

> *They value their parents and think of them as friends.*

4. *They love technology.*

We've already noted that Millennials' role in shaping tech-commerce is one of the factors that make them an important generation. It's also important to understand that technology is part of this generation's identity. When asked in a survey what

> *When asked in a survey what makes their generation unique, a quarter of Millennials listed "technology."*

Millennial Facts

Seventy-five percent of Millennials said they would sooner give up coffee and tea for a week than wireless Internet access. Eighty-seven percent report that they "need" wireless Internet at school, when eating out, and when shopping. Two-thirds say they spend more time on Wi-Fi than they do watching television, and that it would be "impossible" to maintain relationships with friends and family without wireless access. Seventy percent spend four hours or more using wireless Internet daily.

makes their generation unique, a quarter of Millennials listed "technology." That's much higher than any other generation rated *any* identifying feature. They value their phones, iPods, and netbooks. They spend more of their money on cell phones than others, they are the leading users of social media and social networks, and they are the most likely group to engage in a wide range of online activities. Most have never known a world without technologies that seem remarkable to older generations. Technology is a given for them, they are dependent on it, and they can be impatient in any setting, or even with any person, that is not technologically up-to-date.

5. *They are issue oriented.*

Millennials, more than any other generation, will buy for a cause. At their current life stage, Millennials profess more concern about issues such

Millennial Fact

Mobile phones and mobile technology are the number one monthly expenditures for Millennials.

as environmental and social responsibility than other generations. Global causes such as protecting the environment, stopping climate change, and ending poverty are more important to them than to others. They have a positive view of the role of government in society and the economy and are optimistic about the ability of government and activism to change the world for the better.

> *They have a positive view of the role of government in society and the economy and are optimistic about the ability of government and activism to change the world for the better.*

They have a more liberal or tolerant view of social issues like same-sex marriage and marijuana legalization than other generations. This means that Millennial consumers will buy from brands and companies that "take a stand" or contribute to a cause. Conversely, they will have a dim view of businesses that appear callous or reckless toward their community or the environment.

6. *They are peer and group oriented.*

Peer-to-peer recommendations and word-of-mouth are always important in marketing and selling, but especially so for Millennials. They rank peers as their number one source of information in many important product categories. They value their friends. They are attuned and responsive to the tastes

Millennial Fact

Millennials are the generation most likely to volunteer and to buy products that are associated with a cause or charity.

and opinions of members of their group—they want to have what everyone else has.

They seem to act in groups, moving as a herd from one place or product to another. Millennials refer products, brands, videos, web links, Facebook pages, and ideas to one another using texts and social networking. This creates "viral" phenomena in which the attention of thousands, or even millions, focus on the same idea, video, song, or product, in a matter of hours or days. Negative referrals can defuse these phenomena just as quickly as they are created. This means that Millennial consumers are drawn to products and services that seem popular among their peers and will often be more comfortable with sales and marketing when they appeal to a group of their peers.

7. *They value their individuality.*

Although Millennials like to move in groups and are very responsive to their peers, they also feel

Millennial Fact

Peers are the number one source of information about fashion products for Millennials. The Internet is their number one source of information about media products.

Millennial Fact

Twenty-five percent of Millennials have a pierced body part—other than an earlobe.

strongly that they are unique individuals. This may stem from growing up in a world where each person is cherished as "special" and valuable. Whatever the root, Millennials like to proclaim their individuality through their choices in fashion, music, tattoos, piercings, and customizable accessories. They value their identity. Although they want what their peers have, they want it with an "individual" twist, something that makes it their own. Thus, Millennial consumers will be drawn to products and services that can be customized or tailored to recognize their individuality.

8. *They are eager.*

That's actually just a nice way of saying they want it *now*. Millennials seem accustomed to instant gratification. This may stem from the very attentive parenting that many of them received as children. It may also be the result of growing up in a world of fast food, overnight shipping, and instant downloads. Whatever they want, they usually want it immediately. They value their time. They are reluctant to

Millennial Fact

Sixty percent of Millennials are comfortable asking for special treatment.

Millennial Fact

Three quarters of Millennials say they will switch to the competition after just *one* bad customer service experience. Eighty-five percent say they will tell others, likely on social networks.

invest a great deal of time in anything unless it is plainly of value to them. Even then, the window of time may be short. As consumers, they seem to want all purchases to be as simple as a click of a mouse button. If it's more complicated or takes longer than that, they may not stick around. Conversely, transactions that can happen quickly and simply will appeal to them.

9. *They are mostly optimistic.*

For most of their lives, things have gone pretty well. For the most part, when they were growing up, the economy grew, technology became cheaper, smaller, and more powerful, and just about everyone told them that everything they did was super. They believed it. They are generally inclined to think things are going to work out in their favor. As a result, even during the recession, many Millennials have declined entry-level work because they believe something better is right down the road. The post-2008 economic climate may severely test this attitude, but they likely don't want to hear the words, "Sorry, buddy. This is the best you're going to be able to do."

10. *They are ambitious but sometimes directionless.*

Millennials have always been told they could be or do anything they set their mind to. As a result, they

Millennial Fact

Seventy-six percent of Millennials believe they will be better off next year.

can be very ambitious with their aspirations—they often shoot for the moon. However, they may not have enough life experience to know what it takes to shoot for the moon. Or they may not realize that just because their parents told them that they could be astronauts, that doesn't mean they will be allowed to bypass NASA training and shoot straight for the moon.

11. *They are busy and stressed.*

Everyone and everything is competing for Millennials' attention. A typical Millennial has over 500 "friends" on social networks. Many of them send 100 text messages a day. They have spent their lives on busy schedules, bouncing from school to soccer practice to online video games to saving the world. They want and expect the retail experience to be instant and easy.

Millennials steer clear of experiences that are inflexible and intrusive and that take up time. For example, Millennials are the least likely to watch television programs on a TV according to the programmer's schedule. They are the most likely to watch TV programs on the Internet, at their own convenience.

Millennial Fact

Millennials have an average of $19,000 in college debt.

Millennial Fact

Forty percent of adult Millennials still receive money from their parents or family.

Likewise, the use of cell phone *voice* minutes is *declining* among Millennials. Phone calls are too time consuming and intrusive. They vastly prefer texting, which they also can do at their own convenience.

12. *They were raised as their parents' friends.*

Like Generation X, they were raised more as their parents' friends than as subordinate children. As children, their parents made it a point to spend "quality time" with them. As young adults, they are likely to be consulted by their parents for advice.

> *As young adults, they are likely to be consulted by their parents for advice.*

They tend to treat people from all generations as equals, even older generations. They are not disrespectful, nor are they deferential. They are not accustomed to being "spoken down to." When making big purchases, it's not unlikely that Millennials will consult their parents, or even bring them along. Along the same lines, Millennials are quite likely to influence older generations in their family to buy products and services that they like, and to be consulted by their parents about purchases, especially of technology.

13. *They have been well cared for and programmed.*

Through most of their lives, Millennials have been carefully cared for, scheduled, and programmed. They are used to parents and adults in their lives working out all the difficult details for them. If they have moved past one item on the agenda, they are ready for someone to announce what the next step is. They will expect

> *They will expect their retail experiences to be orderly and tidy and without loose ends.*

their retail experiences to be orderly and tidy and without loose ends. They will accept guidance that gets them where they want to go.

Businesses that are interested in the economic potential of Millennials must somehow understand and make sense of their traits and tendencies. Members of older generations risk losing potential connections with Millennial clients and customers by approaching them in the same way they approach older consumers, and those lost connections will translate into lost sales. However, knowing how to approach and appeal to Millennial clients can not only improve sales performance, but can also create a relationship between your business and the twenty-first century's most important group of consumers. In the next chapter, we'll show how to use this snapshot to recognize your potential Millennial customers and how to use the right generational selling tactics to help close the deal with them.

CHAPTER 5

Selling to Millennials

The Search for Connection

Millennial Consumers

Millennials don't have as much accumulated wealth as Baby Boomers or Matures or as much earning power as Generation X—yet. They have yet to reach their earning prime, and many still rely on their parents for financial support. Millennials are just now entering the workforce and the marketplace. However, they will be very influential consumers over the next few decades as they progress in their careers and inherit their parents' assets. As Millennials move up through the business ranks, their buying power and habits may change; however, they will likely remain grounded in a search for a connection to their peers and the greater community.

Millennials are already an important demographic. While they are at the beginning of their earning curve, they are the largest generational cohort, and their spending power is approaching $1.5 trillion per year. In some markets, like small consumer electronics, they already dominate the marketplace. In short, they are worth your attention right now.

Millennials are avid consumers and enjoy the sales process. They want to feel good about their purchasing decisions within their peer group and on a global scale. As we saw in Chapter 4, Millennials are very peer oriented. They move and operate within peer groups—they like to stay with the "pack" or the "herd." When visiting traditional retail outlets (so-called brick-and-mortar stores), they often shop with groups of friends. Online, Millennials have an average of 500 "friends" in social networks with whom they share brand preferences and purchasing decisions. In fact, brand preferences are often part of Millennials' online identity. A recent survey found that over 90 percent of Millennials express brand preference, their fondness for and loyalty to their favorite brands, in their online profiles—just as often as they discuss their ethnic identity or religious preference! The same survey found that three quarters of Millennials discuss brand preference with peers regularly. One-third said they had recently bought a brand recommended by a peer, and the same number said they would not buy a brand that met with peers' disapproval. They also look for the approval of the global community: they are the most likely generation to buy products that are associated with a charity or a worthy cause, such as the environment, global warming, or world hunger.

> *A recent survey found that over 90 percent of Millennials express brand preference, their fondness for and loyalty to their favorite brands, in their online profiles—just as often as they discuss their ethnic identity or religious preference!*

At the same time, they have always been told that they are "special, unique, and different from everyone else." They often want the same things their friends have but still want it to be somehow unique—they want to fit in but be an individual within the group. They value and express their individuality freely and want their purchases to reflect that individuality. And they want to know why products and services are relevant for them personally, as in, "Why is this important to me right now?" They will be responsive to others who notice their individuality, seem impressed by it, and are sensitive to their individual needs.

As a whole, Millennials have not had much prac- tice being decisive. They may know what they

As a whole, Millennials have not had much practice being decisive.

want and are capable of finding tons of information about it from peers and the Internet, but have little experience with the purchase process and the decision to buy. They will respond well to those who act as trusted advisors or guides to help them achieve their goals. They will appreciate sales or account professionals who act as a resource for them for advice and information. Generally, Millennials do *not* lack confi- dence. They are ambitious, and they know what they like— they just need a little help to make their dreams a reality.

Millennials are adept at all communication technology. In fact, they are dependent on it. They are the most likely generation to use text messaging and social media. They are accustomed to their text messages and e-mails being acknowledged or answered instantly and are daily users of social networking. Millennials would rather give up just about anything but their wireless Internet access. In a recent survey, 75 percent of U.S. Millennials said they would sooner give up coffee and tea for a week than their Wi-Fi, and 87 percent reported that they *need* wireless Internet at school, when eating out, and when shopping. Two-thirds reported that they spend more time on Wi-Fi than they do watching television. The

Two-thirds reported that they spend more time on Wi-Fi than they do watching television.

same number of them say it would be "impossible" to maintain relationships with friends and family without wireless access. They are the "digital natives," completely comfortable with all the benefits and pitfalls of technology and can be impatient with sales professionals who don't appreciate the efficiencies offered by these tools. They expect to be able to find a wireless Internet connection for their portable devices wherever they go. If they can't find one, they are likely to be disappointed and look for one someplace else.

In short, Millennial consumers are connected—connected to their peers, to their community, and to the global community, as well as connected by technology to a world of information, entertainment, and commerce like no generation before. In all of these connections, they are attempting to assert their individuality and to stake out their identity. Shopping and buying are important ways for Millennials to both stay connected and express themselves. Sales professionals who understand these Millennial traits and respond to them will have an advantage among what will become the most important retail demographic sector of our time.

> *In all of these connections, they are attempting to assert their individuality and to stake out their identity.*

Identifying and Understanding Your Millennial Customers

Casual dress

Tattoos and piercings

Portable technology

Always texting

Shop with a "pack"

Consult with parents

Need Wi-Fi

Impatient

Like freebies and giveaways

Issue and cause oriented

Like alternative foods and beverages

Style and design conscious

Casual language

If you would like to know if Millennials are patronizing your business, you can use some of the easy market research techniques outlined in Chapter 1. Again, if you have existing paperwork with customer age data, you can simply analyze and categorize it. If you need to gather the data from your customers, methods that utilize technologies like texting and social media will appeal most to Millennials. Also, methods that involve free giveaways or promotions will also appeal to them. If you'd like to know if Millennials are generally interested in your products and services or have the potential to be, you can use the Internet and association resources outlined in the first chapter.

To Do

Use our basic market research techniques to learn about your Millennial customer base and its potential. For the Millennial market, high-tech approaches will work best.

Identifying Millennial customers when they are right in front of you shouldn't be that difficult. Unless you are selling toys or other products for children under 10 years old, Millennials are your youngest customers. They are between 10 and 30 years old and they usually look their age. The oldest Millennials might be hard to distinguish from young Generation Xers, but you can look for signs of the Millennial mind-set if you are unsure. Learning to identify Millennials will also give you some insight into their likes and dislikes

> *Learning to identify Millennials will also give you some insight into their likes and dislikes and their consumer preferences.*

and their consumer preferences. Here are some clues that will help you spot them and understand them as consumers:

- *Casual.* Millennials usually have an ultra-casual approach to fashion, wearing T-shirts, flip-flops, and loose-fitting clothing for almost any setting or occasion. Popular Millennial fashion items are often manufactured and retailed prewashed, prewrinkled, and pretorn. Their T-shirts, brand new ones, are often "vintage" style, made to look like they've been stuffed in someone's drawer since 1976. Pants may appear to have waistbands two sizes too large. Hair may or may not be washed and combed. Don't take it personally. They might show up the same way for a date or a job interview.

- *Tattooed.* They are the most likely generation to have tattoos and piercings. Forty percent of them have tattoos, and 20 percent of them have more than one. A quarter of them have something pierced besides a woman's ear. For older generations, tattoos and piercings might have been signs of a life at sea or a lifestyle from a different part of town. However, if you see a teen or a 20-something with tattoos and a nose or other ring, do not draw any socioeconomic conclusions other than that they are a fairly typical Millennial.

- *Wired.* They sport small consumer electronics, like iPods and smartphones, as fashion accessories. They may still have the earphones or "earbuds" in their ears while they are talking to you. They may be constantly fidgeting and pressing buttons on their phones and MP3 players while you are talking to them. Do not be alarmed. They do the same thing when speaking with their teachers, parents, and bosses.

- *Texting.* They exchange dozens to hundreds of text messages per day, so they are likely to be looking down and typing with their thumbs in the midst of whatever else they are doing. Millennials will not interrupt their texting for you. They are having multiple ongoing conversations via text message all day long. They prefer texting because it allows them to do other things while they communicate—and they will. Again, don't be insulted.

- *The "pack" or the "herd."* They shop with groups of friends and/or communicate with friends while shopping. Millennials have been acclimated to being around peers since their time in day care. They socialize in groups, as opposed to on dates. They find strength in numbers and comfort in staying with the herd. They shop in packs.

> *They find strength in numbers and comfort in staying with the herd. They shop in packs.*

If they are not physically with friends, then they are likely to be in constant virtual contact with them, mostly through text and instant messaging. They will seek the approval of their pack for their purchases.

- *Parents as advisors.* They may also shop with parents and/
  or communicate with parents while shopping. Remember, many Millennials were raised as their parents'
  friends, and they exchange advice both ways with
  them. Millennials and their parents may ask one another for buying advice. Millennials will often involve
  their parents in "adult" purchases like cars, real estate,
  insurance, and financial services. Their parents, in turn,
  will consult their Millennial children when purchasing
  technology or communication products and services.

- *Wi-Fi.* They are always looking for a wireless (Wi-Fi)
  network connection. They typically have a smartphone,
  a notebook or netbook computer, or an iPad or tablet
  device that requires a wireless connection to the Internet. They are adept at finding places that have Wi-Fi so
  that they can stay connected.

- *Impatient.* They are in a hurry—not for any particular
  reason; they just like things to be quick and easy.
  Attention span may be limited to the length of a typical
  YouTube video. They are accustomed to quick and easy
  online communication and commerce and think all of
  life should work the same way. If something takes more
  than a few minutes, they are going to be wondering
  what's taking so long.

- *Something for nothing.* They are attracted to offerings
  that are free or near free. When Millennials were teens,
  they got in the habit of downloading what-ever music and mov-

  > *They are attracted to offerings that are free or near free.*

  ies they wanted from the Internet for free. When they
  finally adapted to paying for music, it was to pay 99
  cents for a song on iTunes. They got their first credit

card in college because the card came with a free T-shirt. When dining out, they select from the dollar menu.

- *Social responsibility*. Their clothing or accessories may advertise their concern about the environment or other causes. Issue advocacy is part of the Millennial style. Although their support for various worthy causes has translated into very little action, they lead the way in advocacy. They wear their advocacy, literally sometimes, on their sleeves.

- *Red Bull, vitamin water, and whole foods*. They favor food and beverages that offer added benefits, like energy drinks and health foods. Caffeine-infused beverages and foods that are ostentatiously labeled "organic" are Millennial fashion accessories. They've been told all of their lives that soft drinks and junk food are bad for them. The alternatives they've chosen aren't always healthier, but they are different, and many of them give the appearance of being more wholesome through packaging and marketing.

- *Style*. Their main interests are technology, fashion, music, and social consciousness. They like clothing and accessories that are unique, quirky, even "dorky," and hip. Yes, for Millennials, quirky and dorky are often the same thing as hip.

> *Yes, for Millennials, quirky and dorky are often the same thing as hip.*

- *LOL*. They communicate informally, both verbally and in writing, even with people they do not know. They often use the same kind of language they would if they were texting, omitting formalities and words they deem unnecessary like articles or determiners. They use more abbreviations and exclamation points than all of the other generations put together. "LOL" is short for "laugh out loud" and is one of thousands of texting abbreviations used by Millennials. It usually means "just kidding" or "that's funny."

- Using these clues, along with what you know about their characteristics from Chapter 4, you should be able to identify customers that fit the Millennial description, if you don't already know their age. Once you know you're working with a Millennial customer, you can use the appropriate tactics.

As we've seen, earning likability and respect from customers is key to successful sales. And earning likability and respect begins with getting your client to listen, to "lean forward." Engaging Millennials and getting them to listen is largely a matter of appealing to their generational sensibilities. Here are some ways to do it:

Engaging Your Millennial Customers

Be concise.

Be up front.

Be yourself.

Immediate application/Instant gratification

Offer something free.

Utilize technology.

Offer free Wi-Fi.

- *Do it quickly.* Millennials are notoriously impatient. There is a lot of competition for their time and attention. Your opening should quickly and succinctly encapsulate what you can offer them. Remember, they can search for and buy something on their smartphones or laptops in less than a minute. They believe everything should be that quick and easy. Consider the length of a typical text message, Facebook status update, or Twitter "tweet"— about 150 letters or characters or less—and that will give you an idea of the bite-size messages that Millennials like to digest.

- *Be up front.* Millennials may not "stalk" their purchases like Gen Xers, but they are exposed to plenty of information about whatever they are buying, mainly from the Internet, in the form of product reviews and peer opinion. If what you are selling has certain features or lacks others, they are likely aware of it—don't hide anything. Make sure all the relevant information you have is available to them. They will look up what you tell them on the Internet to see if it is true. They might even look up your name.

- *Be yourself.* Along the same lines, do not try to affect a young, quirky, or hip manner with Millennials, unless, of course, you *are* young, quirky, and hip. If someone is "trying too hard" to be young and "with it," Millennials will sense that, get turned off, and leave. Instead, be yourself, be natural, be straightforward, and, at the same time, communicate to them that you understand them and can help them get what they want.

- *Offer instant gratification.* Communicate to Millennials that your product or service can be accessed instantly. If it can't be, describe the ways that they can benefit from it starting today, even if it is merely through peace of mind or by crossing an item off of a checklist. Emphasize how fast and easy the whole process will be. One of the best examples of this approach is Volkswagen's "Sign and Drive" promotion in which driving away in a new car can be as simple as signing your name. Your service must have an immediate application and offer instant gratification.

- *Give it away*. Millennials love free stuff. Give them something for free, or close to free, if at all possible. Offer a free sample or a free session or a steep discount. Enable them to access or try your product or service without financial obligation. Offer the first item for $1. Remember, this is a generation accustomed to buying songs and software for 99 cents each. Before that, they were accustomed to getting music and movies for free from Web sites like Napster. They are attracted to the prospect of something for nothing.

- *Go high-tech*. Make sure your Web site is up-to-date, well designed, and full of information that will help Millennials research and find your products and services. Set up a Facebook page and a Twitter feed for your business. Offer coupons, promotions, and updates via text message. Post YouTube videos that tout your business, products, or services. If possible, Millennial customers should be able to buy your products online. If not, perhaps they can reserve what they want or make an appointment via e-mail, text, or instant message to purchase it or meet with you.

- *Wi-Fi*. Offer free wireless access in your place of business. Everyone expects coffee shops to offer Wi-Fi. Millennials expect it to be everywhere else, too. In a recent

To Do

Offer a free wireless Internet connection at your place of business. Millennials expect to find one everywhere, especially when they are shopping.

survey, when asked what they would most like in a car dealership, Millennials responded that they want Wi-Fi access *at the dealership*. In other words, while purchasing a car, or anything else, Millennials would like the ability to turn on their laptops or smartphones and find product research, reviews, and comparisons or to consult peers or parents about their decision *while they are making it*.

Building Sales Relationships with Millennial Customers

Recognize their individuality and accomplishments—build up their self-esteem.

Be a trusted guide who helps them make a decision that is good for them.

Actively manage your reputation.

Use peer testimonials whenever possible.

Associate your products and services with social responsibility and charitable causes.

(*continued*)

(*continued*)

Adapt to Millennial communication and technology preferences.

Offer unique and customized "one-of-a-kind" solutions.

Appeal to the herd mentality.

Keep offerings current and very up-to-date.

Use technology to allow Millennials to freely interact with your business at their convenience.

Once you have gotten your Millennial customers to lean forward and listen, the next step is solidifying your connection with them—building a relationship. Some sales may take minutes, while others will play out over weeks, but in either case, after you have Millennial customers' attention, you can earn some likability and establish a connection that will lead to a sale. Like Gen X, Millennials will screen you before doing business. But once you're on solid footing, your knowledge of your client and his/her world will pay off in many ways and for a long time. Spend time getting to know them. Here are some approaches that will help you build sales relationships with Millennials:

- *Recognize their individuality*. Build rapport with Millennials by recognizing their individuality and accomplishments— build up their self-esteem. Admire them

  | *Admire them as individuals.* |

  as individuals. Say something like, "I'm impressed by you," or "You seem to know your stuff." Let them know that you notice their individual style, that the way they express

> **Do:** Point Millennials to the best places online to research your products and services.
>
> **Don't:** Leave it to chance. You should assume that Millennials will research products online before buying, but you can't assume they will find or use the Web sites that you want them to.

themselves, whether through music or fashion or cause, is distinctive and striking. Say something like, "That's a really unique iPhone app—I've never seen that one before," or "I can see you're very concerned about the environment (or other social cause on their T-shirt). I admire your commitment." At the same time, be careful not to make any comments about appearance that seem intrusive, judgmental, or inappropriate ("creepy," in other words).

- *Be a trusted guide.* Be a trusted guide who helps them make a decision that is good for them. Spend time with them. Get to know the individual. Answer questions. Become a nonstressful resource who is going to help them get what they want. Say something like, "If you're interested, I'll be happy to walk you through this and show you how it works," or "I can show you some Web sites that have some great info on these products." There are a lot of resources available for product research and comparison, and Millennials will be looking at them. Get out in front of that process by suggesting the ones that are the most

> *Become a nonstressful resource who is going to help them get what they want.*

> **Do:** Actively manage your reputation among Millennials, both in person and on social networks.
>
> **Don't:** Ignore the potential damage from a Millennial sharing a poor customer service experience with 500 of their Facebook friends.

even-handed or favorable to you. Let them know that they can text, e-mail, or call you, without obligation, anytime they have a question or hear some confusing information.

- *Reputation management.* Manage your reputation among Millennials. Millennials are acutely aware of what others have and are doing. If their peers have patronized your business, they are likely to be aware of their peers' experiences with you. They will share this information on social networks and other media with hundreds of friends. Again, get out in front of this process by acknowledging it. You might ask them if any of their friends have done business with you and if they were completely satisfied. Say something like, "Have any of your friends used our service? What did they like or dislike about it? I want to make sure we get everything just right here." Millennials are more likely to share private information with one another. This generation regards personal information much differently than older generations. They share information more freely and may know the "nitty-gritty" details of

> Millennials are more likely to share private information with one another.

their friends' business—so be ready to comment (or defend yourself) on them.

- *Peer testimonials.* Peer testimonial is critical. They want to feel good about their decisions within their peer group. If you have Millennial customers or employees who can attest to the quality of what you offer, bring those testimonials into your sales relationships with Millennials. Pass along snippets from texts, e-mails, and Facebook comments (with permission) from satisfied Millennial customers. Millennials put great faith in peer-to-peer referrals. If you have some successful relationships with Millennials, ask them if they will speak to others about you. It will mean a lot. You could offer to put them in touch with one another: "I know some folks in very similar situations to yours who worked with us and are very happy about it. I could put you in touch and they could answer any questions you have about us."

- *Social consciousness.* Millennials will be interested in companies, products, or investments with altruistic aspects, such as environmental or social consciousness. They are the most likely to buy products or services that advertise their commitment to charitable or similar causes. If your business participates in any fund raising for or donations to charities (many do) or any socially or environmentally beneficial programs, make sure your Millennial customers are aware of it, even if

> *If your business participates in any fund raising for or donations to charities (many do) or any socially or environmentally beneficial programs, make sure your Millennial customers are aware of it, even if it is just a recycling program.*

To Do

Associate your company with community service, charitable causes, sustainability, and social and environmental responsibility.

it is just a recycling program. You might say something like, "Our company is committed to this community. That's why our employees do hours of community service and we donate a percentage of our income to community charities," or "We take sustainability very seriously. That's why all of our products are certified as energy efficient and all of our packaging is recyclable." Millennials want to know that they are making socially responsible purchases and investments. It makes them feel better about themselves and is something that they will relay to their peers.

- *High-tech communication.* Millennials have distinct communication and technology preferences. They like to communicate using text messages, instant messages, social networks, and e-mail, pretty much in that order. They are not particularly fond of talking on the phone or going to a lot of meetings, both of which they find time consuming and intrusive. They are accustomed to their text messages and e-mails being acknowledged or answered instantly and are daily users of social networking services. Effective communication with Millennials will involve some or all of these technologies. Technology is assumed and valued and is not feared. If you are entering a sales relationship with a Millennial, it is

To Do

Learn how to use text messaging, Facebook, and Twitter. These technologies are already as widespread as e-mail and Web browsing.

important to learn their preferred method of communication and to make it clear that you are comfortable with technology yourself. Consider asking: "What is the best way for me to contact you or update you? I'm pretty good with most of the technologies available, so I'll use what you prefer." Do *not* overwhelm them with pushy or unwanted messages of any kind, which they regard as "spam" and a misuse of the technology they regard as their own.

- *Individualism*. This is the most individualistic generation—they are uniquely individualistic within their herds, odd as that may seem. Millennials prefer products, services, and solutions that are unique in some way to them. They want what their friends have and want to do what their friends are doing, but they want it to have a unique twist. In some cases, you may be able to offer a standard product that is slightly customized in some way, or you may be able to build a solution just for them. To best develop rapport and give them confidence in you, consider saying something like, "I'm sure there are some things you feel strongly about that set you apart. Let's make my services work for you specifically," or "If we tweak this offer a little, you will have something really unique." Marketers and advertisers are already targeting Millennials with phrases such as "personally yours," "make it your own," and "as special as you are." Try to incorporate these approaches into your sales relationships with Millennials.

- *Herd mentality.* Keep in mind that Millennials move in packs, so target them as a herd. If you can get in front of a group of them, they'll likely think of you when deciding to buy. Consider this approach to a Millennial: "If I buy lunch for you and your buddies, would you invite them to join us for a quick tutorial? No sales, no pressure, no expectations—just an education so you'll be a smarter consumer." Similarly, if you can identify popular Millennials—the leaders of the pack—winning them over will go a long way toward winning the approval of the group.

> If you can get in front of a group of them, they'll likely think of you when deciding to buy.

- *Buzz factor.* Millennials are most interested in what is current—what is hot or "viral" or has "buzz" right now. Make sure what you are offering is up-to-date and not yesterday's news. What was popular a couple of years ago is probably irrelevant to them now. Be certain that you are on top of the latest trends in your industry because Millennials will be. Even what would appear to other generations as fairly up-to-date can be labeled "sooo 5 minutes ago" by Millennials. Technology promotes rapid changes in products and services and rapid awareness of those changes—and that awareness spreads among Millennials faster than any other generation.

- *Online presence.* Use technology to help maintain your sales relationships with Millennials. Make sure that Millennials can "visit" you, your business, and their

To Do

Update your company's Web site and Facebook page to ensure that they are well designed, informative, useful for product research and comparisons, and enable your Millennial customers to contact you and buy from you.

accounts anytime they want, virtually or electronically. They have come to expect that any kind of information should be available to them at any hour of the day from any-where. Configure your company's Web site so that Millennials can

> *They have come to expect that any kind of information should be available to them at any hour of the day from anywhere.*

reach you or your business anytime they want to review products, check account balances, compare prices, look up your bio, leave you a message, download a video, buy something, share it on Facebook, and so on. If they want to virtually revisit your product and you at 2:00 AM in their dorm room and tell their friends about it on Twitter, make sure they have the ability to do just that.

The Last Look: Closing the Deal with Millennials

Like Generation X, Millennials will not respond well to pressure, pushiness, or hard selling. Rather, you should continue to use the same approaches you used in engaging

> **Do:** Be a trusted resource that helps Millennials get what they want.
>
> **Don't:** Use pushy sales techniques or hard sells.

them and building a sales relationship with them. Millennials will not react well if your approach changes suddenly at the close of the sale. In other words, don't build your relationship with Millennials by honoring all of their preferences only to revert to a typical closing strategy at the end of the process. This will have the feel of "bait and switch" to them.

> *Millennials will not react well if your approach changes suddenly at the close of the sale.*

However, when they are making the decision to buy, Millennials will be open to:

- Advice from a trusted source
- Reinforcements from peers and parents
- Reassurances that what they are buying is unique, current, and socially responsible
- Buying options that are fast, easy, and convenient

Putting all these elements together will help move Millennials toward the final purchasing decision. But Millennials want to feel like that purchasing decision is theirs and theirs alone.

Millennials are a virtually cashless generation. They buy using debit and credit cards, online accounts and memberships, text messages, and smartphones. Make sure as many of these options are available as possible. Products and coupons should be available instantly as downloads or through online accounts, if possible. Products that ship should ship practically overnight and preferably for free. Even complex purchases should feel as simple as the click of a mouse or phone button.

Affordability is also key, and initial interaction with the product or service should be free of charge or obligation, if at all possible. Successful Millennial marketing often gives away products with the aim of driving consumers to fee-based products and services. This is true of music, video, print, and software products, which have had the most success in online distribution. Young consumers will want to hear, read, watch, visit with, and use the product before buying or upgrading for a fee.

> *Young consumers will want to hear, read, watch, visit with, and use the product before buying or upgrading for a fee.*

Millennials will expect that the relationship they have developed with you and your business will continue after the sale, as long as they need it to. They will expect the postsale relationship to be as simple, straightforward, and affordable as the sale itself, with instant availability of customer service, unconditional returnability, and continued commitment to the causes and issues that attracted them in the first place.

Remember, Millennials are avid communicators. They are the most likely to tell their peers about their purchases and their favorite companies and brands. And when they tell their friends about their retail experiences—good or bad—using social networks, they are usually talking to about 500 of them at once. The

> *The potential for referrals is stunning.*

potential for referrals is stunning. And the potential of Millennial consumers over the next few decades is not something any sales professional can afford to miss.

For Further Thought on Your Millennial Customers

1. If you're a parent of a Millennial, some of the easiest and least expensive research you can do is to watch your kids and their friends. Ask them why they buy what they buy, why they go where they go, and why they like what they like. Notice if they frequent the same retail stores, and go there and try to see the place through their eyes. Take note of your kids' shopping and buying habits, and bring those ideas to your own place of business.

2. Millennials are very peer oriented, and it is worthwhile to consider them if you need to bulk up your sales staff so that you'll have peers selling and serving peers. They trust one another a bit more, they "click" with one another, and, like all generations, they tend to want to do business with one another. But the Millennials are the newest to the workplace and are often risky new hires due to their history of high turnover. Getting them on your staff, though, so they can serve and sell to their peers might be a good decision.

3. Adjusting to appeal to this generation of 85 million people is certainly a smart decision, but be careful of going too far to accommodate them. It can look phony. More importantly, though, if any of the other generations are the majority of your customers,

changing your look too radically may alienate the ones who are paying you for what you do. Changing too much too fast may make the Millennials look askance at you, and you may end up losing your best clientele, who have been your customers for a long time already. Small, incremental, and nonrisky change is the best way to begin. Once started, gradually build on it.

Takeaways

Millennials will buy products and services:

- That help them feel connected to their peers and to the global community
- That help them find their identity and express their individuality
- From a trusted, nonstressful resource, not a pushy salesperson
- That have an immediate application
- When the sales process is casual, quick, and easy, not fussy, formal, and complicated
- When the sales process utilizes the latest technology
- That are endorsed by their friends and/or parents
- That are current and have the buzz or viral factor
- That are relevant to them as individuals
- Where they can access a Wi-Fi network

CHAPTER 6

Snapshot of Generation X

Meet Generation X

Members of Generation X were born between 1965 and 1979 and now number nearly 60 million. They have often been stereotyped as "slackers" and characterized as unmotivated, lethargic, sarcastic, and irreverent. As youth, they were told that they would be the first generation in the nation's history that would not be better off than their parents. While institutions like government, church, and employer remain important sources of authority for older generations, to Gen Xers they have never

> While institutions like government, church, and employer remain important sources of authority for older generations, to Gen Xers they have never been deserving of anything but skepticism.

been deserving of anything but skepticism. They don't believe they can rely on these institutions—or anyone else—for their well-being, security, or future. So they focus on the short term and what they can get out of today. They are not at all irresponsible, though. Gen Xers have a "find it or do it yourself" attitude and willingly shoulder responsibility for their well-being; they don't trust anyone else to provide it.

Gen Xers were tagged as "slackers" when they first reached adulthood as they postponed careers and marriage for extended stays in college, backpacking around Europe, or hanging around in their parents' houses longer than previous generations. They seemed reluctant to embrace the traditional paths to success and careerism established by generations before them. Their innate skepticism and cynicism may have been part of their reluctance to embrace the "American dream." However, we can see now that their postponement of the traditional milestones of adulthood was simply part of a larger trend. Beginning with the Baby Boomers and continuing right through the Millennials, successive American generations have spent more and more of their 20s in college and in their parents' homes; have delayed career, marriage, and childbirth later and later; and have clung to some "adolescent" ways of life through early adulthood and beyond.

As it turns out, as Gen Xers have matured on their own time and started careers, they have become a dependable, hardworking, and well-educated part of the workforce. Currently in their 30s and 40s, Gen Xers are approaching their peak earning years and are beginning to assume positions of leadership in the business and political worlds. They are a small generation compared to the Boomers before them and the Millennials after them. However, they remain a very important market demographic, with spending power of over $1.5 trillion annually. They are the first tech-savvy generation. They were witness to the birth of the personal computer (PC), the cell phone, the Internet, cable TV, and the World Wide Web, and are an important sector for online commerce. They remain guarded and protective of their own well-being and security and are, quite frankly, some of the toughest sales prospects in the marketplace.

If the Boomers revolutionized popular culture and permanently oriented the marketplace toward youth, perhaps

Generation X Fact

Sixty-five percent of Generation X is currently employed in full-time jobs—the most of any generation.

Generation X has done the most to change the way we all do business, especially in sales. As a generation, they are practically salesproof. Already skeptical and cynical from disappoint-

> *As a generation, they are practically salesproof.*

ing generational and personal formative experiences, Gen Xers were then exposed to an overdose of sales pitches on radio and television. They were the first generation to be raised by television, so to speak. With the advent of cable TV in their youth, they have been exposed to every kind of pitch, promotion, and gimmick in the book.

> *In the popular culture of their youth, from movies like* Glengarry Glen Ross *to TV shows like* The Simpsons, *salespeople are portrayed as desperate and dishonest.*

They are not impressed. In the popular culture of their youth, from movies like *Glengarry Glen Ross* to TV shows like *The Simpsons*, salespeople are portrayed as desperate and dishonest. Their basic approach has been, "If someone is trying to sell me something, why should I believe a word they say?"

In addition to this cynicism and skepticism, Gen Xers are generally very educated. Again, this is part of a larger trend. Before them, the Boomers were the best-educated generation, then Gen Xers became even more educated, and now Millennials are surpassing both in terms of number of years spent in high school and college and number of degrees.

Educated consumers are more capable of finding, reading, and understanding product research, reviews, specifications, and comparisons than older generations. And, because they are avid users of the Internet, they are able to avail themselves of more product information than has ever been available, and they do. This approach has forced retail and sales professionals to be much more "up front" than they might have been in the past—to reveal more and conceal less, to make available as much information as possible. When customers know, or think they know, as much about products and services as sales professionals, full disclosure becomes the best approach to sales. The Gen X approach, skeptical and informed, along with the explosion of online commerce and product information on the World Wide Web, has permanently altered the relationship between salesperson and customer.

> *When customers know, or think they know, as much about products and services as sales professionals, full disclosure becomes the best approach to sales.*

Generation X: The Demographics

Born: 1965–1979

Population: 60 million

Spending power: Over $1.5 trillion annually

More educated and diverse than previous generations

Highest current full-time employment of any generation (65 percent)

Who Is Generation X?

Members of Generation X are the children of the Silent Generation (b. 1925–1945, the youngest generation of the Matures) and the Leading Edge Baby Boomers (b. 1946–1954, the oldest segment of the Baby Boomers). Demographically, Generation X represents the end of the Baby Boom, literally. Pharmaceutical research and changes in the law in the mid-1960s made birth control, especially the birth control pill, widely available. Shortly thereafter, birth rates began to decline, signaling the demographic end to the period of high birth rates that gave the Baby Boom its name. Today, Generation X numbers about 60 million in the United States. Members of Generation X are approaching an age (they are in their 30s and 40s) when they will assume some leadership in their spheres of influence—in politics, in the workplace, in the community, and in major industries. Among them are the founders of Google, Dell, and Yahoo!; prime minister David Cameron of Great Britain; athletes like Tiger Woods and Lance Armstrong; and box office draws like Matt Damon and Gwyneth Paltrow.

Generation X can be difficult to pigeonhole. For example, despite their reputation as disengaged "slackers," they are more conservative on many issues than generations before them or after them, perhaps an outgrowth of their skepticism. Despite their perceived lack of ambition, they have generally excelled in their careers and professional fields. And though they are conservative, cynical, and skeptical, they have embraced some recent trends like environmental awareness and organic foods. They embrace

They embrace technology almost as much as Millennials, but are mainly interested in its practical use, not its faddish appeal.

What's in a Name?

Generation X got its name from a 1991 fictional novel, *Generation X*, written by Canadian author Douglas Coupland. Also known as the Baby Bust, the MTV Generation, and the 13th Generation.

technology almost as much as Millennials, but are mainly interested in its practical use, not its faddish appeal. They embrace sarcastic and ironic humor, but insist on authenticity, facts, and truth everywhere else. They can spot a phony a mile away.

Why Are They Called "Generation X"?

Generation X was first known as the Baby Bust. Like the Baby Boomers, they got that name from the demographic facts. In this case, they represented a decline in birth rates after accessible birth control slowed the Baby Boom. Later, as children, they were often known as the "latchkey kids" (more on that later). When cable TV became widespread, they became known as the MTV Generation, after the music video channel that targeted their demographic. It was a nickname promoted by the network itself. In the landmark book *Generations*, authors William Strauss and Neil Howe applied the label "the 13th Generation" to them because they are the 13th generation in American history. Around the same time, in 1991, Canadian author Douglas Coupland published a fictional novel about the lifestyles of young people in the 1980s entitled *Generation X*. That's the name that stuck and is now the most commonly accepted label for the generation born between 1965 and 1979.

When Were They Born?

Short answer: 1965–1979. In 1964, birth rates returned to their pre–Baby Boom levels, marking the end of that demographic trend, so 1965 is the most logical starting point for the next generation, Gen X. Some demographers pinpoint the end of the Baby Boom around 1960, when Baby Boom birth rates began to decline from their peak, but that is not as widely accepted. For this generation's ending dates, some pick 1977, when birth rates began to inch up again. Others choose dates as late as 1980 or 1981, when the increase in births became substantial and sustained. For ease of use, we stick with the most widely accepted dates that most surveys and studies are based on: 1965–1979. You may see studies and articles that use slightly different dates, and even different names, but we are all talking about the same thing: the group of people born between the mid-1960s and the late 1970s that most people call Generation X.

Formative Experiences

Members of Generation X grew up in a world that had been reshaped by the Baby Boomers before them, in a culture dominated by the Boomers. They were exposed—many of them would say to the point of nausea—to the Boomers' ideals, music, fashion, and fads throughout their youth. Along the way, they noticed that the lofty rhetoric of that era—world peace! free love! no nukes!—didn't exactly

Generation X: The Formative Experiences

Baby Boomer pop culture

Watergate

Inflation

Iran hostage crisis

Gasoline shortages

Early 1980s recession

MTV and cable TV

Space shuttle *Challenger* disaster

AIDS

Iran Contra

Late 1980s/Early 1990s recession

Persian Gulf War

The VCR and the CD player

The PC, the Internet, and the World Wide Web

pan out as advertised. Instead, Gen Xers felt that they got a steady diet of disappointment. For starters, their parents were

> *Instead, Gen Xers felt that they got a steady diet of disappointment.*

more likely to be divorced than any previous generation of children. On a national level, they grew up watching Watergate hearings and American hostages in Iran. The decades-long postwar economic growth slowed to a crawl, first with the inflation crisis of the 1970s and then the recession of the early 1980s. The pain of these changes was felt acutely while they waited in long lines with their families for gasoline in the shortages of 1973 and 1979.

As children during this time, Gen Xers were often known as "latchkey kids." Because of high divorce rates among their parents, and because changing economic times increasingly made it necessary for both parents to work, Gen X kids were often left to fend for themselves. Many returned home from school to empty homes and let themselves in with a "latch-key" hidden under a mat or in their schoolbags and cared for themselves for a few hours until everyone got home. Because of the decline in birthrates, Gen Xers had fewer siblings than older generations. The term *latchkey kids* and its definition paints a kind of sad and lonely picture that is certainly part of the Generation X experience. However, some psychologists have suggested that kids who care for themselves develop more independence and self-reliance—and those are definitely Gen X traits.

> *However, some psychologists have suggested that kids who care for themselves develop more independence and self-reliance—and those are definitely Gen X traits.*

The disappointments continued as Gen X grew up. Most Gen Xers can tell you where they were standing when the space shuttle *Challenger* exploded in 1986. It was a disillusioning failure in what was supposed to be a never-ending march forward in progress and technology. Shortly after that, the government became embroiled in the Iran-Contra scandal, and the stock market crashed in 1987. After they spent the booming 1980s in high school and college, they were told, as they were about to graduate, that there would be a recession and there would be no jobs. Just about the time Gen Xers were old enough to, *ahem*, experience the Boomer-led Sexual Revolution, the AIDS crisis suddenly made sex

> *Around this same time, economists and commentators delivered the foreboding news that this would be the first American generation to be less well off than their parents.*

scary and life threatening. Around this same time, economists and commentators delivered the foreboding news that this would be the first American generation to be less well off than their parents. Who can blame them for taking a few years off, passing the time in grad school and entry-level jobs, or backpacking to Prague?

By the late 1980s and early 1990s, so-called "grunge" music came to embody the spirit of Gen X. Groups like Nirvana and Pearl Jam scored hits with their MTV audience with hard-edged music, slacker-style clothes, and ironic lyrics. One Nirvana song became the unofficial anthem of the generation when it expressed both the blasé attitude and "put up or shut up" approach of Xers in the line "Here we are now, entertain us."

In reality, Generation X did use its independence and downtime to educate and entertain itself. Before the Millennials, Generation X became the most educated generation in American history, in per-capita degrees earned and years spent in high school and college. They also plunged themselves into media, availing themselves of cable TV's new smorgasbord of music videos, reruns, sports, and news. They grew up with TVs in their bedrooms, with CD players, and with VCRs, and they knew how to set the VCR timer—even how to set the VCR clock. They taught themselves how to use PCs, newly available to individual consumers, and even how to program them. As Internet use became more widespread, they embraced e-mail and then the World Wide Web. They became the first media- and tech-savvy generation. Like Gen X hero Quentin

---

Generation X: The Life Stage

Members of Generation X are in their 30s and 40s. They are advanced in their careers and are moving into leadership positions. They have started families and are buying big-ticket items. The average home-buyer is a member of Generation X. If they haven't already, members of Generation X will soon need to begin to prepare seriously for retirement.

Tarantino, they are often walking encyclopedias of popular culture.

Some members of Generation X were finally in the right place at the right time during the technology boom of the 1990s. They were still young but filled with tech know-how. Small Web start-ups turned into multimillion-dollar businesses, fueled by the imagination, tech-savvy, and hard work of Gen Xers. Alas, for Gen X, the tech boom turned out to be a bubble. The days of leaving college early for six-figure salaries went away as fast as they had come. Many Xers had to return to more typical educational and career paths. Still, companies like Dell, Google, and Yahoo! are the legacies of that era and, to this day, Gen Xers still dominate information technology (IT) departments, where sarcasm seems like a job requirement.

Why Is Generation X Important?

1. *They are entering their earning and spending peak.*

   Members of Generation X are entering their peak earning and spending years. Now in their 30s and 40s, Gen Xers are well on their way down their career paths. Well-educated and tech-savvy, they have proven themselves diligent and valuable employees and are moving into leadership positions. Over the next two decades, they should make and spend more money than at any point in their lives.

> *Over the next two decades, they should make and spend more money than at any point in their lives.*

They are raising families and making big-ticket purchases. The average homebuyer, for example, is a member of Generation X. Over the next few years, they will be essential consumers in almost every category.

2. *They lead the way in online commerce.*

While Millennials are usually thought of as the most tech-friendly generation, Generation X approaches, equals, or surpasses them in almost every category. Members of Generation X are the most likely to buy something online and to bank online. This means that Gen Xers will continue to be avid consumers of technology products and services. It also means that, as online commerce is incorporated into almost every business and sales model, Gen X will be one of the principal target demographics for that commerce.

3. *They are planning for the future.*

Members of Generation X are approaching the age when they need to plan for retirement and financial

Generation X Fact

The average homebuyer is a member of Generation X.

Generation X Fact

Members of Generation X are the most likely to buy something or bank online.

security. For account executives and advisors who work in the field of banking, investments, retire-

> *Members of Generation X are approaching the age when they need to plan for retirement and financial security.*

ment planning, and retirement services, Generation X will become the most important market as Baby Boomers move into retirement.

4. *But they still live for today.*

Generation X has always had a *carpe diem*, or "seize the day," approach to life. They don't count on the future and they like short-term rewards. As employees, they are known for their insistence on work-life balance. They don't mind working, but they also want to enjoy their lives right now. This means that, as consumers, they are more predisposed to spend rather than to save. They would rather go ahead and

> *This means that, as consumers, they are more predisposed to spend rather than to save.*

treat themselves to the best consumer products—once they have assured themselves about their quality—than postpone gratification for another day. In other words, if you can get through the sales obstacle course they set up for you, they actually want to buy.

5. *They are loyal customers.*

Once products, services, and brands get the Gen X seal of approval, members of Generation X will stick with it. Once they've gone through the research and trouble to determine a product's quality, authenticity, and value, they are not inclined to go elsewhere. If they find a sales professional they feel they can trust, it's not worth their time to put another one through the trials. Again, if you can get through to Gen X, you will likely have repeat customers.

6. *They are the toughest customers.*

As in the song "New York, New York," if you can make it with Generation X, you can make it anywhere. Generationally speaking, there are no tougher sells in the marketplace.

> *Generationally speaking, there are no tougher sells in the marketplace.*

No customers will demand more of sales professionals in the way of specifications, disclosures, and proof. They will test your patience and your ability to read prospects—to know when to help and when to back off. As we mentioned, they are worth it. They will have money to spend and are willing to spend it. But they will make prospects from other generations seem easy by comparison.

To expand on this a bit, you might think of Generation Xers as "O negative" consumers. In medicine, people with O negative blood type are universal donors, able to donate blood to recipients of any blood type. Xers grew up in a Boomer world but usually act more like Millennials, and they are familiar and comfortable with the people and cultures of both generations. More importantly, though, if you can establish a sales process and environment that satisfies Generation X, chances are it will satisfy demanding consumers from any generation. You will still have to use different generational sales tactics—more guidance and handholding for some, more assertive or familiar approaches for others—but if your sales environment, process, informational literature, and openness work with Gen X, it will be good enough for the rest.

Characteristics of Generation X

Sixty million strong and more diverse than any generation before them, Generation X can present many different faces. Their priorities have changed over time as they have

---

Generation X: The Characteristics

"Prove it or lose it" attitude

Have built-in phony detectors

Educated and tech-savvy

They don't buy, they stalk their purchases

Carpe diem approach to life

Don't trust authorities

Don't have shared heroes

Disdainful or resentful of Baby Boom generation

Raised as parents' friends

Felt like a burden to their families

---

matured toward middle age. Still, surveys and studies reveal some consistent traits that generally do apply, and knowing those traits is important to understanding Generation X's behavior as consumers. Here are some key Generation X characteristics:

1. *Prove it or lose it.*

   The sale, that is. Ever skeptical and cynical, they will not believe any claim or slogan until they see it

   > Ever skeptical and cynical, they will not believe any claim or slogan until they see it backed up with cold, hard facts.

   backed up with cold, hard facts. They've heard countless pitches and jingles and promises and don't think there's anything to back them up. This applies to sales professionals, employers, politicians, and everyone else. If someone makes a claim or accusation or even just e-mails an interesting story, you can be sure that Xers will head straight for snopes.com, factcheck.org, Wikipedia, or Consumers Union to verify whether it is true. They take nothing and no one at face value.

2. *They can spot a phony a mile away.*

   Because Xers insist on the truth, the whole truth, and nothing but the truth, there's no sense in giving them anything but the straight dope. If they have the sense that someone is less than completely honest with them, they will write that person off for good. For most of Generation X, the novel *Catcher in the Rye* was required reading in school. In that book, the worst thing anyone could be was a "phony." They internalized the message, and it was then reinforced by countless episodes from Watergate to Monicagate.

Generation X Fact

About 90 percent of Generation X uses the Internet regularly.

Obviously, no scrupulous salesperson or public official or employer sets out to deliberately deceive people. But the bar is set higher for Gen X. If you don't tell them everything they should know right at the outset, they will assume you are hiding something from them.

> *If you don't tell them everything they should know right at the outset, they will assume you are hiding something from them.*

3. *They are educated and tech-savvy.*

Members of Generation X are more educated than any generation before them, measured in the number of degrees and number of years spent in high school and college. Although the Millennials are on course to surpass them, just as they surpassed the Boomers, their level of education is relatively very high when compared with the rest of the population. This means they are able to find, read, and understand a great deal of information about their intended purchases and to educate themselves about products, services, and industries. By the time they are ready to buy, they will assume they know more about the

> *By the time they are ready to buy, they will assume they know more about the purchase than the salesperson selling it, until proven otherwise.*

Generation X Fact

The founders of Dell, Google, and Yahoo! are members of Generation X.

purchase than the salesperson selling it, until proven otherwise.

4. *They don't buy, they stalk their purchases.*

Along the same lines, Generation X is not inclined to simply go out and make an impulse purchase when the need or desire arises. Rather, they will stalk their purchases. They will look up the products, the reviews, and the recalls. They will "Google" the salesperson and the store. They will ask peers for opinions. They will visit showrooms and stores, often multiple times, and compare prices. At the end of this stalking process, they will decide what they want and whom they want to buy it from. Once they are satisfied they have all the data they can gather, and find a product and a seller they are satisfied with, they will strike quickly. The sales process is over at that point. They just go out and acquire the targeted purchase as swiftly and painlessly as they can.

> *Once they are satisfied they have all the data they can gather, and find a product and a seller they are satisfied with, they will strike quickly.*

5. *They have a carpe diem approach to life.*

After growing up in an era of disappointments and broken promises, Gen Xers have learned not to count

Generation X Fact

Only 33 percent of Gen Xers expect to receive the Social Security they are being promised when they are of eligible age.

on much in the future. They saw their parents and grandparents devote years to careers and companies, only to be laid off or have their pension programs canceled. Often, the future that was always supposed to be better and better just looked worse and worse. Consequently, they learned that if there's something out there that's good for the taking, do it now. They are perfectly willing to work, but want to enjoy the rewards sooner rather than later. *Carpe diem* means "seize the day," and that is Gen X's approach to life.

> *They are perfectly willing to work, but want to enjoy the rewards sooner rather than later.*

6. *They don't defer to authorities.*

   Countless authority figures have let Generation X down. Beginning with Watergate, the leaders of Generation X's youth have been embroiled in scandal after scandal. In the 1980s, a handful of famous preachers as well as some major churches turned out to be harboring some dark secrets. Product failures and recalls cast doubt on the intentions of manufacturers and corporations. The savings-and-loan collapse made banking seem like a house of cards. As a result, authority figures and those who represent institutions, including sales professionals, are not deemed worthy of automatic trust. The

> *The trust of Generation X is hard earned, and it can be lost in a single misstep.*

trust of Generation X is hard earned, and it can be lost in a single misstep.

7. *They don't have shared heroes.*

Unlike previous generations that grew up with war heroes or heroes that were celebrated by nearly everyone in a limited media environment, Gen Xers draw heroes from all over the map, and they aren't widely shared. With 30 channels of TV, and then 70, and then 200, and then the Internet, Gen Xers became diverse in their interests and their admiration. They've always had much to choose from. At the same time, few national or international figures have emerged that enjoy universal support and admiration. And when they do, like Michael Jordan, for example, today's 24-hour media always succeeds in taking some of the luster off of them by telling us a little more than we really wanted to know. One Gen Xer might have grown up admiring Bob Dylan, another Elvis Costello, another Madonna, and another Kurt Cobain. It's hard to find any universally loved figure that they all agree upon.

8. *They've had enough of the Baby Boomers.*

Generation X was raised in a Baby Boomer world, and they kind of resent it. By the time they were old enough to notice, the Boomers had reshaped American culture in their own image. Popular culture in the 1970s and 1980s all seemed to be created by, for, and about Baby Boomers. In music and movies and on TV, Boomers were promising to change the world for the better, but all they ever seemed to do was make it better for themselves. Xers watched their parents and older siblings go whole hog into fads. First they were flower children, then they had disco fever, then they became urban cowboys. As they aged, they flooded pop culture with Boomer nostalgia. Gen X's resentment of the Boomers comes partly from overexposure and partly from the feeling that, for all of

> *Gen X's resentment of the Boomers comes partly from overexposure and partly from the feeling that, for all of their sound and fury, Boomers actually accomplished very little for future generations.*

their sound and fury, Boomers actually accomplished very little for future generations.

9. *They were raised as their parents' friends.*

Generation X was the first generation where children were raised more as their parents' friends than as subordinates who should be "seen and not heard." With fewer children in each family and most parents at work most of the time, parenting began to focus on spending "quality time" with children to compensate for the lack of family togetherness. Kids were allowed to stay up late to watch TV with their parents or to sit at the table and listen while the adults talked because they hadn't seen each other all day. This may contribute to the Xers' lack of deference to older authorities. They tend to see everyone as equal peers.

10. *They felt they were a burden for their families.*

At the same time, culturally and economically, many Xers were made to feel like a burden on their families. Gone were the days when dad worked all day, mom stayed home and took care of the kids, and everyone joined together for a family meal at the end of the day. Instead, as times got tougher, both mom and dad had to work. Day care services became increasingly common as families tried to figure out what to do with the kids while they were busy. In addition to dual careers, most of the Xers' parents also pursued active social lives longer than had been the norm in the past, leaving even less time for the kids. As their parents divorced, Xers became the subject of custody battles. Their world was not the world of *Leave It to Beaver*; it was the world of *Kramer vs. Kramer*.

While Generation X may seem like a prickly bunch, they really aren't that hard to figure out. They just want the

> *While Generation X may seem like a prickly bunch, they really aren't that hard to figure out.*

truth, the whole truth, and nothing but the truth. The hard part is figuring out how to give them what they want in the way they want it and then answering their questions and challenges with patience and accuracy. The effort is worth it. Gen Xers will have money to spend and are willing to spend it. Moreover, once you connect with a Gen Xer, you will likely have a repeat customer and some referrals. In the next chapter, we'll show you how to spot Gen Xers, how to get them to give you a chance, and how to win them over.

CHAPTER 7

Selling to Generation X

The Search for Truth

Generation X Consumers

Generation X, at about 60 million, is a smaller generation than the ones before and after it, but it will be economically important over the next several decades. Members of Generation X are now in their 30s and 40s and are entering their peak earning years. At work, they have begun assuming leadership and senior management roles. In the marketplace, their life stage makes them a leading or key demographic in the market for real estate, automobiles, appliances, electronics, and financial services, among others. They are getting promoted, buying homes, raising families, buying cars, and investing in their retirements. In short, they have money to spend, they are active in the marketplace, and they are buying now.

> In the marketplace, their life stage makes them a leading or key demographic in the market for real estate, automobiles, appliances, electronics, and financial services, among others.

However, members of Generation X can be your toughest customers. They are cynical and skeptical about just about everything and everyone. Sales professionals are high on that list. At the beginning of the sales process, they are likely to view the salesperson as an obstacle, or even an adversary, between them and what they want. On top of that, members of

> At the beginning of the sales process, they are likely to view the salesperson as an obstacle, or even an adversary, between them and what they want.

Generation X are typically the most well-informed customers. They usually don't just walk in and buy something. Instead they like to "stalk" their purchases. They
visit several stores, they comparison shop, and they do
research online. They gather whatever information they
can find on your product and your industry, as well as your
business and you, the salesperson. Once they are satisfied
they have actionable intelligence, they close in on the
target. With this generation, the sales professional must
be a resource for infor-
mation and a facilitator.
The moment that Gen
Xers feel that they are
being sold something,
they are likely to go elsewhere. Needless to say, pushy
sales and closing strategies are strictly off limits for
Generation X.

> *The moment that Gen Xers feel that they are being sold something, they are likely to go elsewhere.*

Perhaps because they are so uneasy about the sales
process, members of Generation X have become enthusiastic
online consumers. Generation X is the most likely to buy
something or use finan-
cial services online. Buying and banking online
enables Gen X consum-
ers to control the sales process and to combine it with
their research of price comparisons and user reviews. And
they are never put in the position where someone is trying
to sell them something they don't want or need or aren't
sure about.

> *Generation X is the most likely to buy something or use financial services online.*

Online commerce is an area of technology where
members of Generation X are more active and involved
than the younger Millennials. Generation X also leads the
way in using the Internet to read newspapers online, for

health and government services, and in the use of the social network Twitter. In fact, with a few exceptions, Generation X is generally on a par with Millennials when it comes to the use of technology. As computers and other personal technologies became available to consumers in the 1980s and 1990s, Xers were the first to adopt them. They are completely comfortable with e-mail, Web browsing, social networking, and smartphones. They don't use text and instant messaging as much as Millennials do, but they are not unfamiliar or uncomfortable with those technologies. Gen Xers like the speed and convenience of communication technologies as much as Millennials but tend to be a little more understanding and tolerant than the younger generation toward those who have not mastered them yet.

Speed and convenience are high on the Generation X priority list. They are more interested in their time than in business relationships. At work, Gen Xers are known for their insistence on "work-life balance." They view work as something they do that enables them to pursue their personal and family lives and interests. They take a similar approach to shopping and buying: it's something they have to do to get what they want, but they don't want to spend all day doing it. They want it to be as quick and painless as online shopping. Long and complicated sales processes that require a lot of face time or "courtship" are not likely to appeal to them.

Similarly, Generation X has shorter time horizons and a carpe diem approach to life. They prefer to enjoy life today rather than to delay gratification to some future date. This is partly the trademark Gen X cynicism and skepticism at work again. Based on their experience of disappointments, they simply don't trust that rewards that take a long time to develop will ever really materialize. They would

> *They would rather take what they can have right now.*

rather take what they can have right now. Along the same lines, they like to know that there's a backup plan ready in case the initial plan doesn't work. This is a generation that is expecting something to go wrong. They appreciate those who are standing by with another solution when the inevitable failure happens.

Generation X shares some of these characteristics with younger Millennials. Like their younger counterparts, they favor technology, speed, convenience, and straight talk. However, members of Generation X have very little in common with Baby Boomers as consumers. Sales tactics that work with Boomers, like appeals to ego and ample

> *Sales tactics that work with Boomers, like appeals to ego and ample face time, will fall flat with Generation X.*

face time, will fall flat with Generation X. Perhaps because they grew up in a world dominated by Boomers, members of Generation X are actually somewhat disdainful of the Boomer mentality. They do not share the Boomers' optimism or sense of self-importance. They are not nostalgic for their youth or that of the Boomers. This is not to say that they are uncomfortable with Baby Boomers. In fact, they tend to understand and relate to Baby Boomers better than Millennials do. Gen Xers simply have a very different mentality as consumers than the next-oldest generation.

As consumers, members of Generation X are looking for truth and authenticity. Their experiences have taught them that those qualities can be hard to find. They enter the marketplace guarded and skeptical, expecting the worst. They arm themselves with research and brace themselves for disappointment. When they do find what they are looking for, they like to make a surgical strike to capture their prize. They prefer to buy with as little interference as possible. It goes against the instincts and training of

> *It goes against the instincts and training of many sales professionals to stand back and leave the customer alone through parts of the sales process, but that is definitely the right approach with the Generation X consumer mind-set.*

many sales professionals to stand back and leave the customer alone through parts of the sales process, but that is definitely the right approach with the Generation X consumer mind-set. While the Gen X approach may be the most difficult for sales professionals to master, it offers the reward of some of the most loyal consumers in the marketplace. If you can pass the Gen X tests, clear all of their hurdles, and run their gauntlets, you will likely have a customer for life. Once you have proven your authenticity to them and your ability to do things right and quickly, you will earn their seal of approval. It's unlikely they will want to invest the time and effort required to put someone else through the trials. You're the one they feel they can do business with. They will be back, and they will tell others about you.

Indentifying and Understanding Your Generation X Customers

To find out if your products or services appeal to Generation X, you can consult some of the online or trade association resources outlined in Chapter 1. If you'd like to know if members of Generation X are patronizing your business, refer

To Do

Use our basic market research techniques to learn about your Generation X customer base and its potential. For the Gen X market, as with Millennials, high-tech approaches will work best.

to the same section of Chapter 1 for some easy, do-it-yourself market research techniques that either utilize your existing customer information or gather that information through promotions, giveaways, and surveys. Methods that utilize technology will be the most likely to capture results from the younger generations, including Generation X.

Identifying your customers who are members of Generation X when they are standing right in front of you is not quite as easy as with other generations, at least from visual clues. Because they are sandwiched between the two largest generations in the marketplace, it's easy to confuse them with Baby Boomers or Millennials. Older members of Generation X are in their mid-40s. They may be graying around the temples a bit, and exhibit other visual features that might lead you to confuse them with Baby Boomers. Younger Gen Xers are in their early 30s and are just as likely as Millennials to present themselves in T-shirts and flip-flops while furiously sending and receiving text messages. To make it even more difficult, Generation X does not have a shared style. They are a diverse group with diverse and individual senses of style.

Fortunately, Generation X has some of the most pronounced consumer behaviors in the marketplace. The Gen

Identifying and Understanding Your Generation X Customers

Well-armed with product research

Like to stalk their purchases

Ask lots of questions

Usually shop alone

Like boundaries

Tech-friendly

Plain and utilitarian style

X consumer mind-set should be fairly easy to identify once you have engaged them as customers. Here are some of the traits and characteristics that will help you identify them:

- *Well-armed.* One of the surest signs of the Gen X consumer mind-set is a customer who walks into a sales environment armed with data. They are determined product researchers. They will educate themselves on every

> *They are determined product researchers.*

facet of your industry and business, including you, before deciding to buy. They will print out reports from online resources like *Consumer Reports*, ePinions.com, and other sources of ratings and peer reviews. If a product has a fault or has been recalled, they already know about it. They have read the specifications and pricing data. If a customer fits the rough age range of Generation X and walks into your place of business with a sheaf of papers about what he or she wants to buy, you've got a Gen X consumer on your hands.

- *Stalkers*. Typical members of Generation X do not simply wander into a store or office and decide on a whim to buy something. Instead, they stalk their purchases. They will first observe from a distance, gathering as much informa-

> *They will first observe from a distance, gathering as much information as they can from research, reviews, ads, and peers.*

tion as they can from research, reviews, ads, and peers. Then they might visit the object of their desire several times in several loca-
tions to judge its look, feel, and price and to assure themselves that this is, in fact, the one they are looking for. They are ready to buy only when they have completed the stalking process and have their purchase cornered. If a customer calls or visits several times to ask questions and examine products or services, without buying, you are witnessing a Gen X consumer stalking his or her prey.

- *The third-degree*. Members of Generation X are likely to quiz and grill sales professionals like no other genera-

> *They want to know "why" a lot.*

tion. They want to know "why" a lot. Why does it cost
that much? Why is it available only in that configu-
ration? Why is it packaged that way? Why are you so anxious to sell me this? Don't take it personally or as an attack on your company's or your credibility. Gen Xers are naturally suspicious of everyone and everything, and they just want straight answers.

- *Lone wolves*. Unlike Millennials, who shop in packs, Gen Xers tend to act alone. They generally don't shop and buy with friends, family, and parents as much as younger

> *They are on a mission, and they are generally all business.*

generations. They are on a mission, and they are generally all business. Going out to buy something is usually not a social occasion for them; it's a task to be completed. They'd rather do it alone, for the most part. They are accustomed to being left to their own devices and figuring out things for themselves.

- *Boundaries.* Gen Xers are guarded about their personal information and their personal space, and they do not go into retail environments to make friends. For Xers, questions like "How are you doing?" and "Are you looking for something?" are borderline personal inquiries that could lead to hard selling. They might like to know that someone is available to help them, but they are probably not in the mood to answer unsolicited questions. Similarly, they probably won't seem too interested in casual sales chatter or banter about the weather. Again, don't take it personally. They are there on a mission, and that mission is not to make friends with salespeople.

Do: Respect Gen Xers' boundaries and give them the space and the time they need to decide to buy.

Don't: Pressure or prod Gen Xers with questions or aggressive sales tactics.

- *Tech-friendly.* Gen Xers are the original tech-savvy generation. They are comfortable with computers, smartphones, the Internet and the Web, gaming technology, and most of the latest gadgets and gizmos—much more so than Boomers. However, they are not as dependent on technology as Millennials, and they understand that there are some people, mostly older than they, who find the latest technology a little confusing. They appreciate the practical benefits of digital, wireless, and other technologies, more so than their "buzz" or cool factors. Technology is efficient; it saves time and money and makes their lives easier. They prefer to use it wherever they can but, unlike Millennials, probably won't walk out of a store just because they can't pick up a strong Wi-Fi signal. If your business has online product information and shopping and buying options, they will likely be interested in using them.

- *Plain style.* As we pointed out, Gen Xers don't really have a shared style or fashion. If they do have a common style preference at all, it would be modest, sensible, and appropriate. This is a generation that was raised in the fashions of the original *Preppy Handbook*. They generally

---

To Do

Ensure that business has an adequate presence on the Internet. It should allow Generation X customers to research, shop for, and, if possible, buy products online.

don't present themselves in ways that call attention to themselves or that are garish, revealing, ostentatious, or sloppy. Their favorite clothing colors are probably khaki and black. These are obviously broad generalizations, and Gen Xers are diverse and have individual tastes, but a modest and utilitarian style definitely fits the Gen X mind-set.

Using these clues, along with what you know about their characteristics from Chapter 6, you should be able to identify customers that have the Gen X mind-set, if you don't already know their age. Once you know you're working with a Gen X customer, you can use the appropriate tactics.

Engaging Your Generation X Customers

Earning likability and respect from members of Generation X may be one of a sales professional's toughest tasks, but it is worth it. As with other generations, it begins with getting them to listen or "lean forward." Engaging Generation X might require you to be a little more reserved and restrained than you would normally be. This is counterintuitive for many

> *Engaging Generation X might require you to be a little more reserved and restrained than you would normally be.*

salespeople. They are often taught that aggressiveness is rewarded with results. With Generation X, almost the opposite is true. The more "hands-off" and passive you are, the more your Generation X customers will feel that they are in control of the sales process. If they feel pushed or crowded, they are likely to look elsewhere. Here are some

Engaging Your Generation X Customers

Be brief and to the point in your introduction.

Sell the steak, not the sizzle.

List all available options—list everything.

Be authentic—Gen Xers can spot a phony a mile away.

If you say you are an expert, be prepared to prove it.

Peer referrals are golden.

Offer short-term solutions with immediate application.

Offer online shopping and buying options.

ways that you can engage Generation X consumers without scaring them off:

- *Be brief.* Introduce yourself quickly and without fanfare while letting Gen Xers know that you are available if they need something. Avoid probing questions like "What are you looking for today?" Spare them the trouble of saying, "I'm just looking around," because that is what they are most likely to say. Instead, say something like "If you need some more information or help finding something, just let me know." Instead of a long verbal introduction, you might simply hand them a business card and say, "I'd be happy to tell you about what we offer if you're interested."

> *Avoid making them feel watched and pressured.*

Avoid making them feel watched and pressured.

- *Just the facts, ma'am.* Typical Gen Xers have little tolerance for sales talk or small talk from salespeople, at least at the outset of a sales relationship. When discussing products and services with Gen Xers, avoid unnecessary verbiage or fuss. They are skeptical of too much hype or promotion. You need to sell the steak; they are not interested in the sizzle at all. They are interested in the facts: the specifications, the dimensions, the performance, and the like. When selling to Gen X, your job is to inform them, not to sell them. View your encounter as an information exchange, not a sales call. Xers crave knowledge and peer reviews. They will likely find out everything they want to know about your products on their own. Instead of fighting that fact, embrace it. Be prepared to answer "Why?" and to refer them to additional, unbiased resources, including side-by-side comparisons, especially if they are online.

> View your encounter as an information exchange, not a sales call.

- *Full disclosure.* List all the available options, solutions, products, services, and so on. List everything. Don't hold anything back or in reserve. Let them know right off the bat what is available. If they suspect you are being cagey

---

Do: Educate Gen X customers by giving them all the information you have at your disposal in a straightforward manner.

Don't: Clutter the sales process with unnecessary chatter or hype.

> ## To Do
>
> Gather some resources to have ready for your customers with the Generation X mindset: helpful Web sites, product reviews, peer referrals, sales and performance data, and so on.

or if the story changes during the sales process, they will smell a rat. Remember, they are in a sales environment to gather information: What is available? How much does it cost? How does it compare to others? Show them where they can go on the Web to read up at their convenience.

> *If you act as a facilitator for them during this process, they will look favorably on you.*

If you act as a facilitator for them during this process, they will look favorably on you. But if they feel that you are trying to manipulate the information, they will assume you are deceptive, and they will find someone else.

- *Be authentic.* Typical Generation X consumers can spot a phony a mile away. You need to be who you say you are and be able to back up the way you present yourself. If you don't share

> *If you don't share their style, interests, or tastes, don't pretend to.*

their style, interests, or tastes, don't pretend to. When they talk with salespeople, Gen Xers are probably probing for clues to whether or not they can trust them. It is best to avoid all pretense and just be who you are. If they get a whiff of any phoniness, Gen Xers will probably write you off.

- *Prove it.* If you claim to be an expert or an authority, you will need to prove it. It is not taken for granted or assumed. Xers are the most cynical generation, and they do not automatically defer to authorities. They don't trust experts until they prove themselves. And for Xers, the proof will be in recent accomplishments, not in a

> *They don't trust experts until they prove themselves.*

lengthy résumé. Be prepared to answer, "What have you done lately?" You can even preempt the question. Consider saying something like, "If I were you, I'd want to know 'what have you done lately?' Let me tell you about what I've been working on, the kinds of clients I serve, and how I've been able to help them."

- *Peer referrals.* Peer referrals are important to Generation X. Peer-to-peer testimonials—about yourself as well as the products and services—will go a long way toward convincing members of Generation X that you are the person they want to do business with. When you have a good connection with a Gen X client, ask if he or she would be willing to serve as a reference. Then, consider saying to potential clients, "If I were you, I would

> *When you have a good connection with a Gen X client, ask if he or she would be willing to serve as a reference.*

want a referral for a business relationship like this one. I have a similar client, and I can arrange for you to ask her some questions about me and how I work with my clients."

- *Carpe diem.* Carpe diem means "seize the day" or live for today, and that is the Gen X approach to life. They tend to have shorter time horizons than other generations. They look for short-term solutions and achievable goals. They don't want to wait for results. In your pitch, look to the short- and medium-term horizon. Explain how your product will improve their jobs and lives the moment after it is used, as well as a few miles down the road. Address their innate cynicism with backup plans for the inevitable time when a problem arises.

> *Address their innate cynicism with backup plans for the inevitable time when a problem arises.*

Xers expect problems, and they will appreciate your willingness to concede imperfection.

- *Online.* Gen Xers aren't as addicted to technology as Millennials, but they are the leading online buyers. Your business should have an online presence, preferably one that facilitates product research, shopping, and buying.

> *Your business should have an online presence, preferably one that facilitates product research, shopping, and buying.*

Xers are slightly more likely to seek out and find your business, even if they can't find it on the Internet, but, for the most part, they will be frustrated if they can't read about and "interact" with your company on their own, and the way they prefer to do that is on the Web.

Building Sales Relationships with Generation X Customers

Once you've passed the Generation X background check and gotten them to lean forward, listen to you, and take you seriously, you have won more than half of the battle. The next step is to build a relationship with your Gen X client or customer to ensure you are the "go-to guy" when they want to buy and that you get the last look for the sale. Some sales are simple and quick, like those in brick-and-mortar retail environments. Others are more complicated, such as in financial services, and play out over a long period of time. In any case, there are some simple ways to cement your relationships with Gen X consumers. Once they are satisfied with a sales experience, members of Generation X can become the most fiercely loyal customers and a great source of referrals. Here are some suggestions for building sales relationships with members of Generation X.

Building Sales Relationships with Generation X Customers

Gen X often values time more than money. Honor that value.

Offer a range of options, not just the popular or promoted ones.

Have a Plan B ready in case Plan A fails.

Allow Gen Xers as much involvement in the sales process as you can.

Use the efficient forms of communication that Xers prefer.

Educate them about your industry, products, and services.

> **Do:** Make your sales interactions with Gen Xers quick, efficient, and convenient.
>
> **Don't:** Use sale approaches that require a lot of face time or "courtship" like golf outings or long meetings.

- *Time is money.* Actually, many Gen Xers value their time more than money. Generation X probably won't want to be courted. They are more interested in their time than in business relationships. To become their vendor or advisor, prove your ability to do things right and quickly, not by spending an afternoon on the golf course with them. When meeting with a Gen X client or prospective client, consider saying something like this: "I know you're busy. Let me show you how well we can perform for you. What interests you about what we offer? Let me come back and show how you'd benefit from our services. It will be quick and to the point. If you like it, we can talk about the next steps." If there's a quick and easy source for your information online, let them know about it.

- *Options.* When you offer Xers a single solution, they may suspect that (1) you offer this to everyone you meet regardless of their needs or (2) there is an internal promotion and you'll sell this regardless of whether I really need it or not. Therefore, you need to offer options. Make sure they have the full range of alternatives available to them. Consider saying something like: "Here are some solutions for you

> *Make sure they have the full range of alternatives available to them.*

> **Do:** Offer your Gen X clients plenty of options, alternatives, and fall back plans.
>
> **Don't:** Try to steer or corral Xers into the most popular or heavily promoted solutions.

based on our discussions of your needs. I've highlighted those that I think fit you and I'll explain why, but here is the entire list for your review."

- *Plan B.* Backup plans are more important to Gen Xers than others. They expect things to fail and plans to fall through. What will happen if Plan A doesn't work? Present proposals that have a Plan B ready if needed. There's no need to go into detail; just let them know you have it. Consider saying: "Based on your needs, I've identified some things that I think will serve you well. If these aren't appropriate for any reason, then I have additional ideas, but let's start with these because I think they'll work."

- *Involvement.* Customers and clients from Generation X will want an uncanny amount of involvement in the sales process. They will want to know every detail. They will look over your shoulder while you are entering their data. They will

> *Customers and clients from Generation X will want an uncanny amount of involvement in the sales process.*

want to know about your sales procedures and policies, even how much commission you will make. They will try to read the paperwork before they sign. They will see any step that they don't personally oversee as an opportunity for someone to take advantage of them. Involve them as much as you can in the process. Let them see the nitty-gritty details. When you are limited by company policy in what you can offer, let them know about the policies and why they are in place. If they can manage and monitor the process online, show them how. Gen Xers want to feel like the process is under their control. Let them.

- *Efficient communication.* Members of Generation X don't need or want a lot of face or phone time in their business relationships. They are adept users of communication technology and like to use things like e-mail and smartphones because they are convenient and efficient. Try to accommodate their technology and communication preferences. Again, they are not as insistent as Millennials on using only the latest forms of communication, but on the whole they do prefer them. Ask them how they prefer to be contacted and oblige them.

  > *Ask them how they prefer to be contacted and oblige them.*

  If your business has online shopping and buying options, direct your Gen X customers to them.

- *Educate them.* When Gen Xers are shopping and buying, one of the most valued contributions a sales professional can make is to provide information. Xers crave information. They want to know everything there is to know about a product or service before they buy it. After doing some product research, reading peer reviews, and comparing prices, they may feel they have educated themselves sufficiently. If you can offer them some background, advice, or information that they were not aware of, it will earn you some respect and esteem in their eyes. If you can, share with them what you know, your "insider" information, and your

> *If you can offer them some background, advice, or information that they were not aware of, it will earn you some respect and esteem in their eyes.*

industry and company data, then they will feel that you have let them in on some special intelligence and their quest to be the most informed consumer will be fulfilled.

The Last Look: Closing the Deal with Generation X

Like Millennials, Generation X will not respond well to the hard sell or pushy closing strategies. Rather, you should continue to use the same approaches you used in engaging them and building a sales relationship with them. Continue to be direct, open, helpful, and unobtrusive. They will not react well if your approach changes suddenly during the sales process. In other words, don't build your relationship with Gen Xers by treating them in the manner they prefer at first, only to morph into the salesperson they always feared when the process nears a close. This will seem deceptive to them.

> *In other words, don't build your relationship with Gen Xers by treating them in the manner they prefer at first, only to morph into the salesperson they always feared when the process nears a close.*

After you have provided all the information you have and answered all their questions, leave the ball in the Xers' court. They need space to make a decision. You should let

> **Do:** Let members of Generation X "close" themselves.
>
> **Don't:** Press for a sale by resorting to aggressive closing strategies at the end of the process.

them "close" themselves. If they feel you have been honest and efficient and the deal you are offering is fair and transparent, most of the time they will do just that. It's not the natural approach for sales pros, but it works. Once you have gained respect as an honest and valuable resource, Xers will remain fiercely loyal—as long as you continue to earn it.

> *Once you have gained respect as an honest and valuable resource, Xers will remain fiercely loyal—as long as you continue to earn it.*

Although members of Generation X may seem a little prickly as consumers and adjusting your sales tactics for them can seem like a chore, selling to Generation X actually gives you the opportunity to relax, have fun, and be yourself in a sales relationship. If you think about it, that's all that Generation X is asking you to do. They are not interested in frills, fanfare, or hype. Nor do they tolerate phonies or aggressive sales techniques. Thus, there is no pressure on the sales professional to generate hype or urgency, to make chitchat, or to feign interest in the customer's personal life and well-being. Instead, you can

> *Instead, you can simply talk to Gen X customers about your products and services the way you would to a friend or a colleague.*

To Do

Ensure that your service after the sale is up to the standards of Generation X (and Millennials). Members of the younger generations will switch to competitors after one negative customer support experience. Ensure that doesn't happen.

---

simply talk to Gen X customers about your products and services the way you would to a friend or a colleague. Give them the facts, answer their questions, hand over all the information you have, and let them do the rest.

Like Millennials, members of Generation X will expect you to stand by your products and services and your sales approach once the sale is completed. Both Millennials and Generation X place a high value on responsive and efficient customer service after the sale. Remember that nearly three quarters of consumers from the younger generations will switch to a competitor after just *one* bad customer service experience. And 85 percent of those will tell their peers about it. Considering that those two generations are the most avid users of social networking, this means that they are likely sharing their bad experience with hundreds, if not thousands, in their networks. Gen Xers and Millennials do not have the time, patience, or attention span to tolerate poor service. Your prospects for repeat business and referrals from Generation X

> *Considering that those two generations are the most avid users of social networking, this means that they are likely sharing their bad experience with hundreds, if not thousands, in their networks.*

depends as much on your follow-through as how you handle the actual sale.

Learning to sell to Generation X can often require you to "forget what you know" as a sales professional and take a more restrained and straightforward approach, but it is worth it. Generation X is relatively small when compared to the Boomers and the Millennials. However, their life stage and their earning potential over the next few decades make them an important segment of the marketplace. Once you win them over, they tend to become loyal customers who will refer their peers. And if you can satisfy these demanding consumers, you can probably learn to work with any generation of customers.

For Further Thought on Your Generation X Customers

1. Xers have begun showing up in management and leadership positions. Most notably, they're showing up in the chief financial officer (CFO) offices. Their questioning attitude and their pragmatic approach to life positions them well for this role. Are you noticing this transition? How can you best adjust to a Gen X CFO who may now have buying power over your services?

2. Generation X is not known for their desire to build relationships until after the sale is made. If you're a Boomer salesperson who has become successful by relationship building with your clients or customers, how must you now adjust? If your Generation X prospects keep saying, "Please just e-mail me the proposal. There's no need for us to go to lunch to go over it," what can you do to try and begin this relationship-building process?

3. Many senior organizations have a history of releasing to the customer only the information needed. Too much information, the thought goes, may confuse the customer or give them reason to shop elsewhere. When Xers can't find the information on a product or service they need, they become testy. Ask yourself if there is information that you've traditionally held back and how and where you might now consider putting that information out to your customers.

(Takeaways

Consumers from Generation X will buy products and services:

- When the sales process is straightforward and transparent
- From sales professionals that inform and educate them
- That are referred by peers
- That have immediate or near-term benefits
- That they can buy online
- When they don't feel someone is trying to pressure or sell them
- When they have multiple options and fall-back plans
- When they are done researching, evaluating, or "stalking" their purchases
- From sales professionals who earn their respect and credibility
- When the sales process is quick and easy

CHAPTER 8

Snapshot of Matures

Meet the Matures

The Matures are actually a combination of two generations, both born before 1946. They either fought in World War II or were children during the war. The eldest members of the Matures remember the Great Depression, and their memories of those times have made an indelible mark on them. Of the four generations, the Matures are the smallest in number, at about 40 million. In per-capita terms, they are also the wealthiest. Most of the Matures entered the workforce during or right after World War II and worked for only one company in their lifetime. They stayed with one employer until they retired, and the company rewarded them with a gold watch and a pension. In retirement, they continue to hold to the values they learned in the hardest of times.

The two generations that make up the Matures are the Veterans, born before 1925, and the Silent Generation, born between 1925 and 1945. Although only the Veterans were old enough to fight in World War II, all but the youngest Matures remember the experience of the war years on the home front, if not the actual theaters of war. Most

Matures Fact

Matures have the highest household net worth of any generation.

also remember the deprivation of the Great Depression of the 1930s. The sacrifice, dedication, and unity that those times required became lasting generational traits. Doing your duty, loving your country, respecting authority, and pulling together for the good of everyone are the essential values of the generations that make up the Matures.

> Doing your duty, loving your country, respecting authority, and pulling together for the good of everyone are the essential values of the generations that make up the Matures.

Following World War II, the Mature generations applied their dedication and service to their employers, families, and communities and helped build a postwar America that became the most prosperous and powerful nation in the world. During the Depression, they had learned to scrimp, save, and be careful with their money. During the war, they learned to follow orders and work together for common goals. They carried these lessons into their jobs, their homes, and their neighborhoods. After years of turmoil, tragedy, and want, the Mature generations found the perfect "soft landing" in postwar American prosperity and stability. Most of the Matures were delighted to settle down to quiet lives in the suburbs, earn a decent living in regular, long-term employment, and enjoy the modest fruits of their labors. Life had never been so easy in any of their memories.

There was no incentive to "rock the boat." In fact, just about everything in the Matures' experience encouraged conformity. During the Depression, they relied on the government for jobs and assistance. During the War, questioning authorities would have been tantamount to treason. After

> In fact, just about everything in the Matures' experience encouraged conformity.

the war, during the Cold War and the Red Scare, Matures continued to take their cues from leaders about what was best for them and their security. They responded by getting jobs, buying homes, starting families (they gave birth to the Baby Boomers), and doing as they were told. Men made up most of the labor force, and women generally stayed home to care for the house and children. Respect was earned through long years of experience and hard work, and through service to your country, especially in the armed forces. Anyone representing the government, the church, the military, or other long-standing institutions and businesses were trusted without question.

The TV sitcom *Ozzie and Harriet* depicted the stable and happy life of the ideal traditional 1950s nuclear family. Father worked, Mom stayed home, and the kids got into some mild comic mischief. Not to worry, Dad would straighten it out when he got home and everyone would have a big laugh about it. The *Ozzie and Harriet* formula was replicated in shows like *Leave It to Beaver*, *Father Knows Best*, and countless similar variations. It was the ideal of American life. However, as the children of the Matures, the Baby Boomers, started growing up, they began to challenge the traditional family and community values held dear by their parents. *Ozzie and Harriet*, *Leave It to Beaver*, and *Father Knows Best* lost their audiences in the early 1960s and were canceled.

Matures Fact

Matures are the most likely generation to have been raised by both parents.

A lot has changed since the time of *Ozzie and Harriet*. The Baby Boomers questioned just about every value that the Matures had imparted to them and shifted the generational balance toward the young. The changing roles of men and women and the Boomers' youthful defiance of authority in the 1960s turned the Matures' world upside down. It was a time of pointed generational conflict. Through it all, however, Matures continued to be a "We" genera-tion, to value hard work, sacrifice, and experience, and to trust authorities and institutions.

> *Through it all, however, Matures continued to be a "We" generation, to value hard work, sacrifice, and experience, and to trust authorities and institutions.*

Now, Matures are in their 60s and 70s and beyond. In 2010, the last of the Matures reached the traditional retirement age of 65. About a third of them will continue to work at least five years beyond retirement age and some will work even further—a trend that will continue to grow in the future. Due to improvements in medicine and longevity, they will live longer than previous generations. Already, the fastest-growing segment of the population is age 85 and over! Their children, mostly Baby Boomers and a few older Gen Xers, are in their 40s and 50s. Their

Matures Fact

Matures are the most likely generation to read a daily newspaper and to watch the news on television.

grandchildren are mostly Generation Xers and Millennial, but some may be even younger. They are likely the last generation to enjoy traditional generous retirement benefits. Because of their conservative approach to savings and investments, and because they were already drawing on retirement funds when the 2008–2009

> *Because of their conservative approach to savings and investments, and because they were already drawing on retirement funds when the 2008–2009 recession started, they have not been that hard hit by economic hard times.*

recession started, they have not been that hard hit by economic hard times. The Matures' sense of civic duty remains strong. For example, they are among the most likely generations to vote in an election. They are also the most likely generation to read newspapers and watch the news on television. However, their chief concerns now are enjoying their retirement years, preserving their health and dealing with the effects of aging, and leaving a legacy for their children and grandchildren.

Matures: The Demographics

Born: Before 1946

Population: 40 million

Wealthiest generation, per capita

All Matures are now past the traditional retirement age of 65

Who Are the Matures?

The Matures are made up of the first two generations born in the twentieth century—the Veterans (born before 1925) and the Silent Generation (born 1925–1945). They are the parents of the Baby Boomers and some of Generation X. Today, they number about 40 million in the United States, the smallest of the generations, in part because birth rates in the United States during the Depression and World War II were low. They are past traditional retirement age and are an important market for retirement, aging, and health-related products and services. Notable Matures include former presidents George H. W. Bush and Jimmy Carter, astronaut and senator John Glenn, evangelist Billy Graham, and actors Jack Nicholson and Clint Eastwood.

Matures still believe strongly in "truth, justice, and the American way." They believe their endurance and service during the Depression and World War II has earned them the right to be treated with respect. They believe experience is the best teacher, and they have plenty of it. They are likely to be a little "set in their ways" and expect others they meet, like salespeople, to understand and respect the way they like to do business. At the same time, they don't expect their every whim to be catered to with a customized solution. Standard and prepackaged offerings are fine for them. They believe the most important feature a product or service can have is quality. And they trust testimonials from "blue-chip" sources—major publications and organizations—that attest to that quality. Like everyone else, they don't like to be reminded of their age. Still, their current life stage is the most important factor determining in which markets they will be active.

> They believe the most important feature a product or service can have is quality.

What's in a Name?

Matures is a catchall term to describe the generations born before 1946, the Veterans and the Silent Generation. Also known as Traditionals or Traditionalists. The Veterans are so called because of their service in World War II. Also known as the G.I. Generation or the Greatest Generation. The Silent Generation is known for its conformity.

Why Are They Called Matures?

The term *Matures* is actually a catchall term for the two oldest generations. Sometimes they are known by the similar catchall terms *Traditionals* or *Traditionalists*. The older generation of the Matures, the Veterans, is so called because of the service of many of their generation in World War II. They are also sometimes called the G.I. Generation or the Greatest Generation for the same reason. The younger of the two Mature generations is called the Silent Generation. The term *Silent Generation* was first used by *Time* magazine to describe them in 1951, noting that they were "working fairly hard and saying almost nothing" in contrast to the youth of the 1920s, which *Time* described as "flaming." You may see all these labels used in different publications—Matures, Silents, Veterans, GIs, Traditionals—but most of the same characteristics and generalizations will apply to all of the living generations born before 1946.

When Were They Born?

Short answer: 1901–1945. Some observers date the beginning of the Veterans generation as late as 1905 but, at this point, it's a moot question. The far end of the demographic spectrum—people over 100 years of age—comprises only a tiny percentage of the population. The generational divide between Silents and Baby Boomers has been the subject of a little more debate, fluctuating between 1942 and 1945. However, the U.S. Census has adopted 1946 as the official starting point for the Baby Boom generation and that really decides the issue for Silents, too. In fact, the easiest way to think of the Matures is that they are anyone born before 1946.

Formative Experiences

Matures: The Formative Experiences

The stock market crash of 1929

The Great Depression

The New Deal

FDR's fireside chats

Attack on Pearl Harbor

World War II

The atomic bombing of Japan

The G.I. Bill

The Red Scare

The Cold War

The Korean War

The Great Depression and World War II—that pretty much says it all. Not only were these the defining events for the Matures, they are probably the most important formative experiences of any generation. Not only did the experience of these two events shape the Matures, but they also form a large part of their identity. A recent Pew survey asked each generation, "What makes your generation unique?" The leading response among Matures was "The Great Depression and World War II." Other generations chose characteristics like "work ethic" or "use of technology." The Matures have never forgotten what they went through in those times, and they know those experiences have always been a big part of their generational personality.

> *A recent Pew survey asked each generation, "What makes your generation unique?" The leading response among Matures was "The Great Depression and World War II."*

The Great Depression began when the market crash of 1929 triggered a sustained and painful economic depression. A massive decrease in personal wealth was coupled with a scarcity of jobs, leading to a collapse in consumer demand. Unemployment reached its peak in 1933 at 25 percent, the highest level in the nation's history. Severe drought made matters even worse in the heartland. Hunger and homelessness became commonplace in what had been a prosperous nation just a few years earlier. The song of the decade was "Brother Can You Spare a Dime" because it touched on the difficulties many faced, as well as their dependence on handouts. Following a succession of bank failures, people found it safer to keep what money they had under the mattress rather than in banks. Matures also likely remember

Matures Fact

Sixteen million Matures served in the armed forces during World War II. Almost 1 million of them were killed or wounded during the war.

helping friends, neighbors, and strangers in need. Many came to depend on the government assistance of Franklin Roosevelt's New Deal for survival and on his leadership and "fireside chats" for hope.

It took nearly a decade for the nation to gradually climb out of the Depression. At the end of that decade, the United States was drawn into the global international conflict of World War II. The event that launched the United States into the war was the shocking attack by Japanese planes on Pearl Harbor. Most Matures have vivid memories of that event and commemorate it every December 7 till this day. Over 16 million Americans served in the armed forces during the war and almost a million were killed or wounded in action. Millions more felt the sacrifice as members of servicemen's families. Even those who didn't serve in the military were drawn into the war effort on the home front. Many, including many women for the first time, worked in wartime industries such as munitions factories. Others supported the war effort by buying bonds, volunteering for the United Service Organizations (USO), or collecting materials that were needed for the war. Goods such as gasoline, medicines, and certain foods were rationed to civilians. The entire nation was urged to be vigilant and thrifty. The war was finally brought to a close in 1945 following the massive D-Day invasion of Europe and the atomic bomb attacks on Japan.

Following the war, servicemen returned home with the urge to settle into quiet, peaceful lives. They were encouraged and supported financially by the G.I. Bill and postwar prosperity. However, new threats in the form of the communist Soviet Union and China kept America on guard. Wartime vigilance was replaced by Cold War vigilance. The Red Scare suggested that communist threats also came from within. In many ways, the Cold War kept the Matures on a wartime footing indefinitely. The values of loyalty and patriotism remained as important as they had been

> *In many ways, the Cold War kept the Matures on a wartime footing indefinitely. The values of loyalty and patriotism remained as important as they had been during wartime.*

during wartime. Eventually, the Cold War led the nation into further conflicts in Korea and Vietnam over the course of the 1950s.

In the 1960s, the Matures' children, the Baby Boomers, began to challenge their parents' values. Eventually, the Boomers' own values of questioning authority and "doing your own thing" competed with the Matures' Depression and war-era morals in an era of generational conflict, ultimately drowning out the voice of the Matures' "Silent Majority."

The Matures: The Life Stage

All Matures are now past the traditional retirement age of 65. Although most are retired, about a third will continue to work at least five years beyond retirement. Most Matures are now focused on retirement pursuits, health and aging issues, and their legacy to their children and grandchildren.

The Matures have held on to their values, though, even if those values aren't shared by other generations.

Why Are the Matures Important?

1. *They are the wealthiest generation.*

Although the Baby Boomers have more spending power overall, the Matures have the highest *per-capita* wealth. Put another way, Matures have the highest household net worth of any generation.

> *Put another way, Matures have the highest household net worth of any generation.*

They have money to spend. They have spent their lifetimes in dedicated service to their employers and have been rewarded with pensions and retirement accounts. They may be the last generation to enjoy such generous benefits. They have also been careful stewards of their money through most of their lives. Most of them were already in retirement by the time of the recession of 2008–2009. Because retirement funds are usually moved into conservative investments once retirement starts, they did not suffer the same kinds of losses to their wealth that Boomers did. In retirement, they will finally have occasion to use it.

2. *They are crucial for certain markets.*

For certain categories of products and services, Matures are a key demographic. These include the categories of health, aging, travel, second homes, retirement destinations and communities, and investment products that will benefit their heirs, among others. In addition, Matures will be a strong market for other categories, such as electronics and appliances, when those products are tailored or adapted for ease of use by those with age-related limitations. In still other

> *In addition, Matures will be a strong market for other categories, such as electronics and appliances, when those products are tailored or adapted for ease of use by those with age-related limitations.*

cases, Matures can be a sustaining market for products that don't have the same appeal for younger generations, such as newspapers, products of long-standing traditional brands, and products that are "made in America."

3. *They are loyal consumers.*

Loyalty, quality, and trust are important values to the Matures. If they find a company or a sales professional that appeals to those values, they are going to keep coming back. Once Matures find a product or service that they like and a sales process that is comfortable and easy for them, they are not likely to search for another. Many of them have stuck with one brand or one company in each product category for decades. If

> *Many of them have stuck with one brand or one company in each product category for decades.*

you can make yourself that one person they trust in your industry, you may be able to enjoy their business for years to come.

Matures Fact

The fastest-growing segment of the population is age 85 and over.

4. *They have staying power.*

Modern medicine has produced a revolution in longevity. Over the course of the Matures' lifetimes, average life expectancy has increased by about a year every decade. The average expectancy for someone who is currently 65 is almost 20 more years of life. In fact, the fastest growing segment of the population is age 85 and over.

> In fact, the fastest growing segment of the population is age 85 and over.

Beginning with the Matures, we can expect that those who live to 65 will continue to live longer than previous generations. They are also likely to enjoy a higher quality of life in their senior years. That means many will continue to be active, to work (over a third of Matures are working past retirement), and to participate in the marketplace.

5. *They are easy to reach.*

Matures may be the last generation easily reachable through traditional marketing and retail channels. With Matures, there's no need to figure out which form of modern communication technology they prefer. The tried and true will work fine: newspaper ads, direct mail, television commercials, brick-and-mortar stores, sales calls, and appointments. They are mostly retired so they are not overscheduled or "on the go." You don't have to worry about networking with them on

Matures Fact

One-third of Matures will work at least five years beyond traditional retirement age.

Facebook or getting them to follow you on Twitter. They will respect product

> *In other words, you can sell to this generation the old-fashioned way.*

reviews, awards, and testimonials from established publications and organizations. In other words, you can sell to this generation the old-fashioned way.

6. *They are influential.*

Matures are influential within their families and communities and among other generations. Millennials, in particular, tend to develop strong bonds with Matures. They are respected for their experience and advice by those in other generations who are close to them. In some cases, Matures may be able

> *They are respected for their experience and advice by those in other generations who are close to them.*

to refer you to members of younger generations as sales prospects. Often, Matures are also in the position of providing financial support for their children and grandchildren in younger generations, in which case their input concerning spending decisions will be even more influential.

Characteristics of Matures

Matures: The Characteristics

Sense of duty
Sacrifice and dedication

(*continued*)

(*continued*)

    Loyal

    Patriotic

    Value experience

    Conformist

    "We" first

    Like standard and established offerings

    Value quality

    Set ways

Matures are probably the most homogenous, or least diverse, generational group. Obviously, in a group of 40 million people, there will be differences and variations. But, for the most part, Matures tend to have more similar backgrounds—ethnic, religious, educational, in employment, and in experiences—than younger generations. Almost all of them share the memories of the defining events of their lifetimes—the Depression and the War—and almost all of them were shaped by those events.

7. *They have a sense of duty.*

The Matures' experience of the Depression, World War II, and the Cold War instilled in them a strong sense of duty—to one's country, to one's employer, and to fellow citizens in the community. They appreciate the same sense in others, especially military veterans, long-tenured employees, and those with a record of service to the community. They will respond well to businesses and sales professionals that exhibit those qualities and appear to share those values.

Matures Fact

Matures are the most likely generation to donate to a charity.

8. *They know the value of sacrifice and dedication.*

Matures' experiences have also taught them the value of sacrifice and dedication. For many of them, these qualities were a matter of survival in the hardest of times. They believe that what they have was earned with their own blood, sweat, and tears. They had to endure deprivation and loss and often had to sacrifice their own interests for the good of others and to get where they are. They will appreciate those who understand that they have to work long and hard to earn what they want more than they will those who appear to want everything to come easily.

> *They will appreciate those who understand that they have to work long and hard to earn what they want more than they will those who appear to want everything to come easily.*

9. *They are loyal.*

For the Matures, loyalty has always been an essential quality. To get through the Depression, they had to be loyal to their families and neighbors. To get through the war and the Cold War required loyalty to their country. These are absolute values. A handshake and a promise are

> *A handshake and a promise are pledges of trust for Matures and should always be honored.*

pledges of trust for Matures and should always be honored. A breach of trust or loyalty will cause them to write you off.

10. *They are patriotic.*

Many Matures fought for or served their country in war efforts that were a matter of survival for their country and its values. Many others had family members or close friends who lost their lives in these same wars. They do not take their citizenship lightly or for granted. They have a high participation rate in elections and believe the well-being of the nation is of the utmost importance. They believe that everyone else should feel the same way. They respond positively to symbols and demonstrations of patriotism from individuals and businesses.

> *They respond positively to symbols and demonstrations of patriotism from individuals and businesses.*

11. *They value experience.*

For Matures, experience will always be the best teacher. In terms of years in and degrees from high school and college, they have the least formal education of the four generations. However, they believe they learned more from long years on the job and from their trying experiences than anyone could learn in school. If you have a proven track record in your field, that will count for much more with Matures than any

> *If you have a proven track record in your field, that will count for much more with Matures than any number of degrees.*

number of degrees. If you or your business has many years on that track record, that's even better.

12. *They are conformists.*

Matures don't like to rock the boat and don't think much of people who do. Everything in their experience, from the Depression through the Cold War, encouraged conformity. Seeing later generations question every authority, beginning in the 1960s, was a trying experience for them, and they never lost their sense that "going along to get along" is the best and safest course of action. They respect

> They respect the words of established authorities—political, business, church, and community leaders—and can be suspicious of those who challenge them.

the words of established authorities—political, business, church, and community leaders—and can be suspicious of those who challenge them.

13. *They put "we" first.*

Along the same lines, Matures have always felt that they should do what is best for the group—for their family, their colleagues, their community, their country—over and above what is good for them as individuals. Younger generations have tended to be "Me" generations, and that has been another source of generational conflict. Matures value the team and the group and see those who put their own interests first as selfish and counterproductive.

14. *They like standard and established offerings.*

Matures do not believe they, or anyone else, are entitled to special treatment. On the contrary, they are more comfortable with standard and

> *On the contrary, they are more comfortable with standard and prepackaged offerings.*

prepackaged offerings. Again, they prefer the "tried and true" and don't need something customized especially for them to be satisfied.

15. *They value quality.*

For Matures, the most important feature any product can have is quality. They are generally not concerned whether a

> *A proven track record of quality and reliability will count for a lot more with Matures than slick marketing or branding.*

product or company is trendy or has "buzz." They want to know, "Does it work?" or "Is it dependable and will it last?" A proven track record of quality and reliability will count for a lot more with Matures than slick marketing or branding.

16. *They have set ways.*

Matures have years of experience—of work, of living, of being consumers—and, by now, they have established preferences and ways of doing things that they trust and rely on. They may also have

> *When they are doing business or buying something, they will likely have some "rules of engagement."*

set beliefs about how people should conduct themselves and communicate with one another. When they are doing business or buying something, they will likely have some "rules of engagement." They may expect certain formal courtesies or for the process to unfold in a certain manner. These expectations will vary from person to person, so it is best to ask directly what the "rules" are and then follow them.

While Matures are the smallest of the four generations, they have the highest net worth per household. They are vitally important consumers for many sectors of the market, and they can be influential among consumers of other generations. Matures will also enjoy greater longevity in their lives and in the marketplace than previous generations did in the retirement years. Because of their long experience and unique perspective, Matures may have specific "rules of engagement" for doing business or buying, but it will be worth your while to learn them. In the next chapter, we will show you how to recognize Matures among your potential customers and how to choose the right tactics to best engage them.

Selling to Matures

The Search for Quality

Mature Consumers

Matures are the smallest generation of consumers, at about 40 million. However, because the Mature generation is made up of all of the generations born before 1946, it has the largest age range. Matures may range in age anywhere from 65 to over 100. The older end of that spectrum constitutes only a tiny percentage of the population, but consumers over 85 years of age make up the fastest-growing age segment in the United States. Mature consumers also have the most per-capita accumulated personal wealth of any generation.

Many members of the Mature generation have memories of the difficult economic times of the Great Depression and of sacrifice during the war years. Those experiences made an indelible mark on their families and their mind-set. As a result, many are still very careful and conservative with their financial resources. Those lean years were followed by decades of growth and prosperity, but Matures see that prosperity as a product of their moderation and hard work. They are proud of their country and their contribution to it and believe everyone else should be, too.

Duty and sacrifice are at the heart of the Mature mind-set; accordingly, sales professionals must earn their business. Good intentions, snazzy packaging, and a controlling persona are not generally effective with Matures. Matures usually do not have an inflated ego or sense of self-importance. They don't expect special treatment, but they do believe they have earned a certain amount of deference and respect

> *They don't expect special treatment, but they do believe they have earned a certain amount of deference and respect for all that they have accomplished.*

for all that they have accomplished. They believe that experience is the best teacher and that they have plenty of it. They will respond best to those who recognize and respect their wealth of life experience.

During times of depression, war, and Cold War, members of the Mature generation not only learned to value austerity, but also to respect authority. Religious, political, and business leaders are all sources of authority that Matures respect. They believe that businesses are institutions, like the government and the church, that

> *They are likely to see experienced, knowledgeable, and competent sales professionals who represent businesses as experts or business leaders.*

act in good faith for the benefit of our nation and our communities and are worthy of trust. They are likely to see experienced, knowledgeable, and competent sales professionals who represent businesses as experts or business leaders. For the most part, they will implicitly trust representatives of institutions until they have reason to do otherwise.

They prefer the standard, trusted, "blue-chip" businesses to the novel and faddish newcomers. When given a choice, they will usually stick with the tried and true. If they are unfamiliar with a brand or product, a testimonial or positive review from a recognized and trusted source, like a venerable publication or a trade association, will help them feel more comfortable with it. Again, the opinions of institutions carry weight with Matures. If your business does not yet have "institution" status, it will help if it is endorsed by people or organizations that do.

Matures' deference to institutions is part of their "We Generation" mentality. They value conformity, blending, and unity. They don't believe in "rocking the boat." They believe that rules are important and should be followed, that rules benefit rather than restrict us. Based on their years of experience, they often have a firm idea of what the rules should be. That means most Matures have a set of rules in mind for how they like to do business. Sales professionals need to find out what the rules are and honor them.

The number one rule for Mature consumers as a whole is that they value quality above all else. Does it work? Is it well made? Will it last? Does it do what it's supposed to do? Matures believe they grew up in a time when things were made to last. They don't think that their purchases should become disposable after a few years. They are generally not concerned about whether a product or service offers the "latest," or if it's unique to them. They just want to make sure it's of good quality. Over the years, Matures have developed firm ideas about what constitutes quality. Sales and account executives should seek Mature clients' definition of quality and meet it.

> They don't think that their purchases should become disposable after a few years. They are generally not concerned about whether a product or service offers the "latest," or if it's unique to them. They just want to make sure it's of good quality.

The majority of Matures are already retired, and life stage is a major factor in determining consumer preferences for Matures. If they haven't already done so, they are choosing retirement destinations, whether in retirement communities or smaller, more manageable housing in their own community. They are downsizing and simplifying their lifestyles. They are focused on their health and longevity. They spend more on health services than any other generation. They are also interested in leaving a legacy for their children, their communities, and institutions that are dear to them. In many cases, they already contribute financial assistance to their children and grandchildren, especially for education and major "life" purchases like real estate and automobiles. All of these life stage developments are occasions for spending. Although the Matures tend to spend cautiously and to reduce their expenditures as they get further into retirement, they will continue to shop and buy in the categories that are important to them and from retailers that they know and trust. Businesses that are focused on younger markets might miss out on sales to Matures if their approach to sales and marketing does not match their expectations. By using some Mature-specific selling tactics, you can connect with this important generation of consumers.

> All of these life stage developments are occasions for spending.

Identifying and Understanding Your Mature Customers

To find out if Matures are potential or actual customers for you, utilize some of the simple market research techniques spelled out in Chapter 1. If you have existing documentation with your customers' ages or dates of birth, you can simply analyze and categorize it. If you want to gather the data from your Mature customers, do not rely on technologies like

Identifying and Understanding Your Mature Customers

Age- and setting-appropriate appearance

Like to blend in

Patriotic

Low-tech

e-mail and social networking. You will miss some of your older customers. If you'd like to know if Matures are generally interested in your products and services, or have the potential to be, you can use the Internet and association resources discussed in the first chapter.

Identifying Mature customers who are standing right in front of you shouldn't be too hard. They are all over retirement age, and, unlike Boomers, most have no problem looking and acting their age. They don't dress, speak, and act as casually as younger generations and don't usually feel the need to keep up with the latest fads and fashions. The mindset of the Mature consumer is fairly easy to recognize, too. Here are some ways to spot them:

- *Distinguished.* Matures usually have an age- and setting-appropriate appearance. They grew up in a time when shopping was an occasional and important outing, requiring a trip to a shopping district. Men wore suits and hats, and ladies wore dresses to shop on Main Street. They are no longer that formal, but neither are they in blue jeans or shorts. They might still seem a little overdressed by today's standards, but that's what

> *Most don't feel the need to try to look 20 years younger than they are.*

makes them comfortable. Most don't feel the need to try to look 20 years younger than they are.

- *Conformist.* Matures don't like to rock the boat, ask for special treatment, or proclaim their individuality. When

> *They prefer to blend in.*

they shop, they are usually content to buy what you are offering rather than demanding a custom or unique solution. They prefer to blend in. They don't see "standing out from the crowd" as a virtue but as a sign of self-centeredness and ego.

- *Patriotic.* In general, Matures are proud of their country and their service to it. Many have served the nation in the armed forces or have family members who have. They remember and honor the sacrifice and dedication of everyone who has. They commemorate patriotic holidays and display outward signs of love of country. They believe everyone else should have the same respect, and they notice when others do.

- *Low-tech.* Not surprisingly, the Matures are the least comfortable with technology of all the generations. They generally prefer to communicate in the ways

---

To Do

If Matures visit your office or business frequently, consider displaying a flag or other patriotic symbol in public areas.

Do: Communicate with Matures the "old-fashioned" way, with visits, meetings, calls, and letters.

Don't: Rely on electronic communications like e-mail and texting with Matures unless they ask you to.

that they always have: face to face, by telephone, and by mail. They prefer to read documents on paper rather than on a screen. Some are adopting cell phones and computers and some even go online, but it is not likely that they will adopt these as their primary means of communication.

Using these clues, along with what you know about their characteristics from Chapter 8, you should be able to identify customers that have the Mature mind-set. Once you know

Engaging Your Mature Customers

Introduce yourself.

Respect their experience, dedication, and sacrifice.

Ask for the "rules of engagement."

Emphasize quality with testimonials.

Standard and prepackaged is good.

Don't mention that a product is "good for their age group."

> **Do:** Introduce yourself by name and title to begin your conversation with Matures.
>
> **Don't:** Strike up a casual conversation without letting them know who you are.

you're working with a Mature customer, you can use the appropriate tactics.

Communicating with Matures in the way they expect will help you earn respect and likability. Getting them to lean forward and listen is not that hard. They start out the sales process with respect for you as a representative of your business. In return, they expect you to respect the way they like to do business.

- *Introduce yourself.* Provide Matures with a formal introduction to let them know who you are and what you do. If you have a title, use it. If you have a business card, offer it. Don't simply walk up to them and start a casual conversation. Make sure they know who you are and that you represent the business they have visited.

- *Respect.* You must respect their authority and ask how they prefer to conduct business—asking before assuming will earn trust. They believe experience is the best teacher, and they have plenty of experiences to draw from when making buying decisions. Show that you value what they've learned through experience and all of their contributions and hard work.

> *Chances are, your Mature customers have some built-in rules on how they like to work with salespeople or vendors.*

> ## To Do
>
> Gather some testimonials from respected publications, people, or institutions to share with your mature customers.

- *Rules.* Rules are important to Matures. Chances are, your Mature customers have some built-in rules on how they like to work with salespeople or vendors. Ask for them and follow them. Consider asking this way: "What do I need to know to work with you? Are there any steps you like salespeople to follow? What are the rules I need to follow to have a good working relationship with you?"

- *Quality.* Emphasize quality at every opportunity. Provide testimonials and reviews from trusted sources and publications. Place less emphasis on the bells and whistles. Consider saying something like: "Our company gets super reviews. Here are a few that have been printed recently that I'd like you to see." Ask the prospect how he or she defines success and quality, then identify how your product meets those criteria and back it up with proof. Matures respect proven authorities, so refer to the track record of your product and your leadership.

- *Standard and prepackaged.* Most Matures are perfectly comfortable with standard and prepackaged offerings. They don't require something customized and unique. In fact, they're usually more

> *In fact, they're usually more comfortable getting the same thing everyone else is getting.*

comfortable getting the same thing everyone else is getting. They like the tried and true.

- *Don't mention age.* Never mention that a product is good for their age group. It is a marketing and advertising truth that most people think of themselves as 10 to 15 years younger than they really are. Even though Matures are more comfortable acting and looking their age than, say, Baby Boomers,

> *Even though Matures are more comfortable acting and looking their age than, say, Baby Boomers, they don't need to be reminded of it.*

they don't need to be reminded of it. They don't want to be told, "This is right for you because you're old."

- *Sell.* As with Boomers, Matures are not averse to sales and advertising. Many of them entered the business world by starting in sales, and they see salespeople as professional representatives of their companies. They are accustomed to and comfortable with traditional sales techniques and approaches. The Boomers and Matures will give you the opportunity to sell in the way that you have learned to. Find out what their needs and wants are. Put your products' best features forward. Ask for their business. Ask to move to the next step.

> *Find out what their needs and wants are. Put your products' best features forward. Ask for their business. Ask to move to the next step.*

Building Sales Relationships with Mature Customers

Once you've engaged Mature customers and gotten them to lean forward and listen, you can build on your relationship.

Building Sales Relationships With Mature Customers

Follow the rules.

Deliver the goods.

Stay in touch.

Make it easy for them.

Show your dedication and sacrifice.

Your sales relationship with them may only take a few minutes, it may take a few weeks, or it may be ongoing. In any case, you can cement your connection with Matures with these simple suggestions:

- *Follow the rules.* Make sure that you have specifically asked your Mature customers how they like to do business. Know what the rules of engagement are, and follow the rules faithfully. If, at any point, something unusual happens or you need to step out of bounds, explain to them patiently and carefully what's going on and emphasize that you understand their rules and intend to keep to them.

- *Deliver.* After taking the time to understand your Mature customers' definition of quality, you need to meet that definition. Don't overpromise or fail to live up to a promise. Matures will see that as a breach of trust.

- *Stay in touch.* Keep in contact with Mature clients and customers to let them know you're there. Send cards on holidays, and call them to update them on their accounts. Use the mail for correspondence and supplement that with electronic communication if they indicate that it's OK. Make sure your correspondence is easy to read and understand. Mailings or ads

> *Mailings or ads that include a photo of you do not work with younger generations but are good for reminding Matures who you are.*

that include a photo of you do not work with younger generations but are good for reminding Matures who you are. Patriotic images such as flags or monuments are also appealing to Matures when included on printed materials.

- *Make it easy.* Many things have changed over the course of Matures' lifetimes, and the pace of that change has accelerated over the past few years. Things have become more complicated, not just in technology, but also in many other industries and in business transactions in general. Some Mature consumers may find the new ways of doing business intimidating and confusing. Assist them by making each aspect of the sales process easy to understand and digest. Help them to feel that they are on solid footing and know exactly what's going on.

- *Dedication and sacrifice.* Remember, dedication and sacrifice are important values for the Matures. Let them know that you share them. Let them know how hard you

To Do

Carefully explain complicated sales documents and processes to Mature customers.

are working for your company and community—and not just yourself. Emphasize your institutional history and your number of years of service. If you have any history of military or government service, let them know about that, too.

The Last Look: Closing the Deal with Matures

As with Baby Boomers, closing the deal with Matures can be simple and to the point. Like Baby Boomers, Matures will give you the opportunity to use the selling and closing strategies you have learned to be effective. Once you have established a connection with them based on trust, respect, and likability, they will give you the time and attention you need to make your case. Play by their rules, and prove the quality of what you are offering. Then ask to move to the next step.

After you have demonstrated that what you're offering meets their expectations for quality, close the deal. Summarize their expectations and how you met them, and then ask for the business. The "ask" is imperative with Matures, who continue to expect you to earn their business, even if they are already sold. And once you've earned the trust, respect,

To Do

Ask for the sale.

> *The "ask" is imperative with Matures, who continue to expect you to earn their business, even if they are already sold.*

and business of Mature customers, they are likely to stick with you and tell others about you.

In fact, Matures can be an unexpected source of referrals from younger generations. There seems to be a special connection between the Mature generation and younger generations, especially Millennials. They trust one another and seek advice from one another. Establishing a good relationship with Matures could also give you the opportunity to meet the next generation of clients.

> *Establishing a good relationship with Matures could also give you the opportunity to meet the next generation of clients.*

Matures are a small but significant demographic in the marketplace. They play a role in the purchasing decisions of the young people in their lives, often helping to finance them. They have the highest per-capita net worth of any generation and are crucial consumers for certain industries. They have accumulated that personal wealth through years of dedication and service to their companies and their country. By treating them with the respect and deference that they have earned, and offering the quality they seek, you will make it easy for them to connect with you and, ultimately, to buy from you.

For Further Thought on Your Mature Customers

1. The Matures tend to be the best at interpersonal communication and are being used in many cases as customer service providers. Customer service will

always be very important, regardless of how each generation wants to receive it. Can you make your Matures the teachers of service skills best practices? They often serve as great teachers of the Millennials. And where the Millennials engage other generations to provide service, the Matures will be a great resource of knowledge on how to treat the others.

2. One thing some retail stores have done is to create a gathering place for the Matures to collect and visit with one another. Fast-food restaurants open early to allow the early birds to gather over coffee. Mall walkers finish their workouts and gather in the food court to visit. And where they visit, they buy. Can you create a gathering spot for the Matures and, in return, earn their patronage?

3. The Matures' children can be very involved in their parents' decisions today. The children, often Baby Boomers or Generation Xers, fear their parents being taken advantage of by some slick salesman or confusing contract. Be prepared for someone to be serving as an advisor for the Matures from time to time. They'll be reviewing documents, advising them after the call, or even be in a meeting with them. When that's the case, you need to use the selling tactics for both the generations you're dealing with so that they both feel at ease and confident about you.

4. If the Matures visit you in your workplace, become aware of the little things that will make visiting you easier: chairs with arms to aid in sitting down and standing up, larger and wider pens that are easier for elderly hands to manipulate, larger print sizes for documents, and so on.

Takeaways

Consumers from Mature generations will buy products and services:

- From sales professionals who ask for the "rules of engagement" and follow them
- When their definition of quality is fulfilled by a product or service
- From salespeople who respect their experience and sacrifice
- From trusted "blue-chip" institutions and brands
- From salespeople who communicate with them in ways they are accustomed to
- From among standard and prepackaged options that are "tried and true," not unique and customized
- From salespeople who are like them or who show that they understand them

CHAPTER 10

Closing the Deal

Connecting and Selling across Generational Lines

B y this point, you should be able to understand the challenges posed by selling across generations or, more specifically, the potential difficulty in connecting with prospects from generations other than your own. Regardless of your own generational background, however, with an understanding of each generation's idiosyncrasies, you should be equipped to identify, engage, and build a relationship with each generation of customer.

When it comes to signing on the dotted line, consumers' decisions are based largely on that connection. Closing the deal lies mainly in how the decision maker feels about the process, about you, and about him- or herself. Being aware of the role generational biases play in the process and using

> *Closing the deal lies mainly in how the decision maker feels about the process, about you, and about him- or herself.*

the tactics outlined in this book can help sales professionals stand apart from the crowd and better pave the road to "yes."

The Big Picture

After reading the generational snapshots and tactical guides, you should have a good sense of the importance of generational differences. Generational differences are a fact of life whenever and wherever people of different generations come together. They have an impact on the workplace, the marketplace, and even within families, as well as in society and culture at large. Generational differences can lead to conflict or they can be bridged through insight and understanding.

Taking a broad overview of the four generations, "from 60,000 feet," you can see what the major differences are. The older generations, especially the Matures, tend to be more "We" generations that value what's good for the family, the group, the team, the community, or the nation and that focus on long-term goals. The younger generations, especially the Millennials, tend to be more "Me" generations, valuing the individual and the short term. From the oldest to the youngest, there is a sort of continuum of values from "We" to "Me" that helps shape each generation's behavior as employees, consumers, citizens, and family members.

Thus, Matures and Baby Boomers think of themselves as part of larger groups or units. They value performance and quality over the long run. They esteem organizations with distinguished histories, with name recognition, and with tenure in the marketplace. Millennials and Generation Xers, however, think of themselves as individuals. They are interested in how things will affect *their* lives, in things that make them unique and distinct, and in developments that are happening *now*. This continuum of values from the older to the younger is even visible within the Baby Boomer generation. The older Early Boomers exhibit more of the "We" values, while the younger Late Boomers have some of the "Me" qualities.

Understanding this generational continuum will help you apply generational insight in sales. As we mentioned, birth date does not dictate personality. More than exact age, you want to know where your customers fit on this scale. What is their mentality or mind-set? More "We" or more "Me"? More long-term or more here and now? More often than not, the outlook will fit the generation. In some cases, especially with customers on the "borderline" between generations, you can determine to right approach by figuring out which generational values form the most apt description of the customer in front of you. Think of the generational types of consumers as representative of consumer types in general—types that mostly fit within certain age groups. In this way, generational insight in sales is simply insight that enables you to better read your customers and respond to their needs.

The Details

Now that you have a better understanding of the outlook and behavior of each generation of consumer, you can start implementing approaches that work best for each. Going forward, you should consider how you can implement generational sales tactics in your own sales environment. Here are some questions to consider as you begin to apply these tactics:

1. *What steps will you take to identify and understand the different generations of clients that you serve and sell to?* What tactics will you use to learn about the demographics of your customers? Review the methods we provide in Chapter 1 for learning more about your own customer base, either through information you have on file or through information you solicit from your customers. Also consider using some of the basic market research techniques to learn more about the potential appeal of your business to each generation. As we mentioned, you will find that some approaches work better with certain generations. For example,

gathering data through electronic communication works best with Millennials and Generation X, while more traditional methods work best with Matures and Boomers. When you compare your own customers to the marketplace in general, you may discover some new possibilities for growth among certain demographics. You may also see that you need to enhance your generational appeal to some segments of the market.

2. *How will you distinguish what you offer for each generation?* Each generation is looking for something a little different in marketing and sales. Think about ways that you can portray and present what you offer in a way that appeals to each of the four generations. Consider ways that you can tailor the sales environment and sales processes in order to make each generation a little more comfortable with them. Think about the characteristics and tactics that apply to each generation and how your approach can incorporate them.

3. *What steps will you take to deploy generational selling tactics to the sales floor?* What key insights and tactics do you need to apply to which situations and which customers? What are the best ways to share these insights and techniques with your sales and marketing teams? Consider some ways that you can track your intergenerational interactions and sales to find out which tactics are the most effective for you.

4. *How do you plan to update your information technology and communications?* Up-to-date technology and communications are obviously crucial for selling to younger generations. But even older generations are

increasingly availing themselves of resources like Web-based product research and price comparisons. And even if they aren't, they will often ask their children from younger generations to do it for them. Simple steps like developing a helpful and informative online presence and offering free Wi-Fi are necessities for doing business with Millennials and Generation X and will ultimately pay dividends across the generations. *Hint:* younger colleagues in your business can usually help a great deal with this one.

5. *What steps will you take to manage your reputation among younger generations?* Given the wealth of resources now available for consumers to research your company, your products, and you, you need to know what is being written and said about your business online in reviews, ratings, and social media. Your customers from younger generations will already know, and they will share it with their friends and family from older generations. Learn what anyone can find out when they "Google" your name and the name of your business or product. Take steps to help shape what's written about you on the World Wide Web and know where to guide your customers who want to do online product research. *Hint:* younger colleagues in your business can usually help a great deal with this one, too.

6. *How do you plan to win over younger generations' peers and parents? Older generations' children and grandchildren?* More than ever, different generations of consumers within the same family or circle of friends now advise and consult one another about their purchasing decisions. In one sale, a sales professional can face buyers from multiple generations. Consider ways that

you can simultaneously connect with a Baby Boomer buyer and his or her Millennial advisors/children.

7. *What materials should you prepare to appeal to each generation?* Consumers from Generation X may want to see hard data. Millennials may want referrals from peers. Matures may want to read testimonials from trusted sources. And Baby Boomers may want to see ways that your products can be customized. Consider the needs and wants of each generation and prepare materials about your products and business that will appeal to each in advance.

8. *What new business practices should you consider to appeal to each generation?* Can your business allow for more customization to appeal to Baby Boomers and Millennials? Are there rewards or "trophies" that you can offer to Baby Boomers for their business? Are there aspects of your products or services that can be made available for free to Millennials? Is there "inside" information about your products that you can share with Gen Xers? Can you contribute in some way to a charity or a cause that would appeal to Millennials? Can you honor the nation and those who have served it in a way that would appeal to Matures? Your business model may not currently allow for these kinds of measures, but they come at a relatively low cost. Consider some low-impact changes to your policies and procedures that will help you appeal across generational lines.

Implementing generational sales and marketing techniques is simply a matter of reviewing generational characteristics, preferences, and tactics and incorporating them into your regular business practices. Most of them involve minimal expense and effort but will go a long way toward making a connection across generational lines.

The Crucial Connection

In our high-tech world, tools like the Internet, e-mail, the World Wide Web, and social media should, theoretically, make marketing and selling easier. Sales professionals can now reach more consumers with more messages at a lower cost than ever before, right? In reality, these have become tools that make *buying* easier but *selling* harder. If, as the saying goes, knowledge is power, now most of the power in the marketplace is being transferred to the consumer. Consumers have a wealth of resources at their fingertips. They can compare products and prices, read reviews and ratings, and research companies and the sales professionals that represent them. They can choose when, where, and how they want to buy from among multiple options. Customers can now scan a bar code in your place of business with their smartphones and view a map with the best prices for that product in your neighborhood. In many cases now, through outlets like Priceline and eBay, they are even being asked to name their own price!

> *In reality, these have become tools that make* buying *easier but* selling *harder.*

As a salesperson in this environment, you need to do more than just give customers a reason to buy. You need to give them a reason to buy from *you*. And getting customers to choose to buy from you involves forming a connection with them. In order to stand out from all the options facing consumers today, sales professionals need to achieve a comfort level with their clients based on likability and respect and, of course, avoid turning them off at the start. Customers will respect you for your competence, professionalism, and knowledge of your product and your industry— because you do your job well. How do you get them to like you? Well, that's a little more difficult to put your finger on. But it starts with sending the right signals and speaking the same language. It starts when you send signals to your

> *How do you get them to like you? Well, that's a little more difficult to put your finger on. But it starts with sending the right signals and speaking the same language.*

customers that you understand them and how they like to be approached. That's what gets them to listen. It continues when you speak a common language that allows you to connect with them. Then you are on your way to likability.

It's easier to form a sales connection with people who are like us. We're all more comfortable working with people from our own age and background. In an earlier time, when most of the workplace and marketplace was dominated by one or two generations, it was often possible to do business mostly with people close to your own age. In our own time, that is no longer possible. Consumers from ages 18 to 80, representing four very diverse generations, are fully engaged in the marketplace. In order to succeed, you must be able to connect with them all, and that means bridging generational differences. Selling across the generations requires you to understand people with different generational perspectives, to identify and read their mind-sets, and to respond to them in a way that helps you to form that crucial sales connection. Learning and applying the generational insights and tactics we have presented here will enable you to do just that.

ABOUT THE AUTHOR

Cam Marston led the research and is the voice to the impact each generation has on sales, service, and workplace dynamics. In his research for his corporate and association audiences, Cam outlines nuances and the impact each cohort will have on business and how to best prepare as each generation moves through different life stages. Clients have ranged from Fortune 500 companies to local and regional associations.

Cam's first book, *Motivating the "What's In It For Me?" Workforce* was published by Wiley in 2005. His second book, *Generational Insights*, was released in 2010. Both received extremely positive reviews for capturing, summarizing, and offering solutions for today's intergenerational workplace challenges. His management training videos have been industry best sellers since released.

For more information, contact Generational Insights at www.generationalinsights.com.